D0817009

RESPONSIVE WEB DESIGN
IN PRACTICE

SEP 2 4 2018

Library Technology Essentials

About the Series

The *Library Technology Essentials* series helps librarians utilize today's hottest new technologies as well as ready themselves for tomorrow's. The series features titles that cover the A–Z of how to leverage the latest and most cutting-edge technologies and trends to deliver new library services.

Today's forward-thinking libraries are responding to changes in information consumption, new technological advancements, and growing user expectations by devising groundbreaking ways to remain relevant in a rapidly changing digital world. This collection of primers guides libraries along the path to innovation through step-by-step instruction. Written by the field's top experts, these handbooks serve as the ultimate gateway to the newest and most promising emerging technology trends. Filled with practical advice and projects for libraries to implement right now, these books inspire readers to start leveraging these new techniques and tools today.

About the Series Editor

Ellyssa Kroski is the Director of Information Technology at the New York Law Institute as well as an award-winning editor and author of 22 books including *Law Librarianship in the Digital Age* for which she won the AALL's 2014 Joseph L. Andrews Legal Literature Award. Her ten-book technology series, The Tech Set, won the ALA's Best Book in Library Literature Award in 2011. She is a librarian, an adjunct faculty member at Pratt Institute, and an international conference speaker. She speaks at several conferences a year, mainly about new tech trends, digital strategy, and libraries.

Titles in the Series

1. *Wearable Technology: Smart Watches to Google Glass for Libraries*, by Tom Bruno
2. *MOOCs and Libraries*, by Kyle K. Courtney
3. *Free Technology for Libraries*, by Amy Deschenes
4. *Makerspaces in Libraries*, by Theresa Willingham and Jeroen De Boer
5. *Knowledge Management for Libraries*, by Valerie Forrestal
6. *WordPress for Libraries*, by Chad Haefele
7. *Game It Up!: Using Gamification to Incentivize Your Library*, by David Folmar
8. *Data Visualizations and Infographics*, by Sarah K. C. Mauldin
9. *Mobile Social Marketing in Libraries*, by Samantha C. Helmick
10. *Digital Collections and Exhibits*, by Juan Denzer
11. *Using Tablets and Apps in Libraries*, by Elizabeth Willse
12. *Responsive Web Design in Practice*, by Jason A. Clark

RESPONSIVE WEB DESIGN IN PRACTICE

Jason A. Clark

ROWMAN & LITTLEFIELD
Lanham • Boulder • New York • London

Published by Rowman & Littlefield
A wholly owned subsidary of The Rowman & Littlefield Publishing Group, Inc.
4501 Forbes Boulevard, Suite 200, Lanham, Maryland 20706
www.rowman.com

Unit A, Whitacre Mews, 26-34 Stannary Street, London SE11 4AB

Copyright © 2015 by Rowman & Littlefield

All rights reserved. No part of this book may be reproduced in any form or by any electronic or mechanical means, including information storage and retrieval systems, without written permission from the publisher, except by a reviewer who may quote passages in a review.

British Library Cataloguing in Publication Information Available

Library of Congress Cataloging-in-Publication Data

Clark, Jason A.
Responsive web design in practice / Jason A. Clark.
pages cm.
Includes bibliographical references and index.
ISBN 978-1-4422-4368-2 (cloth : alk. paper) — ISBN 978-1-4422-4369-9 (pbk. : alk. paper) — ISBN 978-1-4422-4370-5 (ebook)
1. Web site development. 2. Web sites—Design. 3. Library Web sites. I. Title.
TK5105.888.C5425 2015
006.7—dc23
2015013754

∞ ™ The paper used in this publication meets the minimum requirements of American National Standard for Information Sciences Permanence of Paper for Printed Library Materials, ANSI/NISO Z39.48-1992.

Printed in the United States of America

This book is dedicated to Jennifer and Piper who have endured and supported me as I slogged through the creative process known as writing.

To Jennifer, I thank you for your incredible patience and support as I found my way. I could not have done it without you.

To Piper, I apologize for the lack of pictures. I think you might have been right when you suggested this book needed more of them.

CONTENTS

SERIES EDITOR'S FOREWORD

Responsive Web Design in Libraries is a start-to-finish guide to creating a responsive Web site that automatically resizes and adjusts itself to the dimensions of the device on which it is being viewed. Jason Clark, the authority on responsive Web design, provides a comprehensive overview of principles such as fluid grids, CSS media queries, flexible objects, and other core functionality inherent to this new but well-adopted standard in Web site design. Clark provides an in-depth walk-through for readers to learn how to retrofit an existing Web site to be responsive, how to create new responsive forms, and how to create a brand new responsive layout from scratch. This essential guidebook simplifies the complexity of designing responsive search interfaces, creating single page applications, and utilizing a responsive framework on a complete Web site.

The idea for the Library Technology Essentials book series came about due to the many drastic changes in information consumption, new technological advancements, and growing user expectations during the past few years, which forward-thinking libraries are responding to by devising groundbreaking ways to remain relevant in a rapidly changing digital world. I saw a need for a practical set of guidebooks that libraries could use to stay on the cutting edge by implementing new programs, services, and technologies to match their patrons' expectations.

Libraries today are embracing new and emerging technologies, transforming themselves into community hubs and places of co-creation through makerspaces, developing information commons spaces, and even taking on new roles and formats, all the while searching for ways to decrease budget lines, add value, and prove the return on investment of the library. The Library Technology Essentials series is a collection of primers to guide libraries along the path to innovation through step-by-step instruction. Written by the field's top experts, these handbooks are meant to serve as the ultimate gateway to the newest and most promising emerging technology trends. Filled with practical advice and project ideas for libraries to implement immediately, these books will hopefully inspire readers to start leveraging these new techniques and tools today.

Each book follows the same format and outline, guiding the reader through the A–Z of leveraging the latest and most cutting-edge technologies and trends to deliver new library services. The "projects" chapters comprise the largest portion of the books, providing library initiatives that can be implemented by both beginners and advanced readers accommodating for all audiences and levels of technical expertise. These projects and programs range from the basic "How to Circulate Wearable Technology in Your Library" and "How to Host a FIRST Robotics Team at the Library," to intermediate, such as "How to Create a Hands-Free Digital Exhibit Showcase with Microsoft Kinect," to the more advanced options, such as "Implementing a Scalable E-Resources Management System" and "How to Gamify Library Orientation for Patrons with a Top-Down Video Game." Readers of all skill levels will find something of interest in these books.

I had the pleasure of working with Jason Clark on a previous book for the Tech Set book series on mobile library applications. Right then I learned that Jason is one of those rare professionals who is incredibly knowledgeable about his area of expertise yet has the ability to express even the most complex concepts in an utterly accessible way. As head of library informatics and computing at Montana State University libraries, Jason is an experienced authority on responsive Web site design and that is evident through his outstanding book. If you're contemplating a Web site redesign for your library, you'll want to add this title to your professional collection.

—Ellyssa Kroski
Director of Information Technology
The New York Law Institute
www.ellyssakroski.com

http://ccgclibraries.com
ellyssakroski@yahoo.com

PREFACE

Today's library patrons are browsing the Web on a variety of devices including tablets, e-readers, mobile phones, and desktops. Responsive Web design (RWD) employs techniques that enable your library's website to automatically adapt to whatever screen size it's being viewed on. In this book, you will learn how to utilize HTML best practices and CSS techniques such as fluid grids and flexible images combined with responsive design techniques such as media queries to deliver an optimal experience for your users regardless of device.

With both beginner and expert developers in mind, this complete handbook guides readers through the process of developing and launching their own RWDs and introduces the craft of building multiscreen experiences. Chapters 1 through 4 introduce the history, context, and first steps for using the RWD development model. Chapter 5 is the centerpiece of the book and focuses on the "how to" with a set of projects ready for implementation, including detailed code recipes and working downloads to get the reader started. Chapter 6 takes a closer look at some tips and tricks that can be applied to the RWD model. Chapter 7 considers emerging best practices and possible future directions for RWD. Finally, chapter 8 looks at recommended reading and further resources for learning about RWD.

A primary goal of this book is to demystify the process behind developing and designing within the RWD model. As mentioned earlier, learning about RWD is the first step and this book covers the history and formation of RWD, how to think about design for the multiscreen setting, possible future trends in RWD, and much more. However, the core of the book focuses on how to build sample RWD prototypes that use library data or that work in a library setting. Specific projects include an RWD retrofit of an existing site, an RWD bookreader interface, a responsive contact form, a single-page application applying the RWD model, a responsive search interface, and a Twitter Bootstrap prototype Web site. In the end, I'm hoping that readers are empowered to create new library applications and services based on the code samples and walkthroughs available here.

ACKNOWLEDGMENTS

I would like to acknowledge the terrific work of Ellyssa Kroski, my editor. Her vision for the Library Technology Essentials series helped frame my writing, her insistence on keeping the projects and writing accessible for a broad audience resulted in a better book, and her patience and consistent demeanor as I struggled with the creative process of writing was much appreciated.

1

INTRODUCTION

Responsive Web Design (RWD) in Practice

1.1 WHAT IS RWD?

At the time of this writing, 2010 was five years ago. What is interesting about these five years is how much has changed in the Web design and development world. We have moved from mobile computing—the ability to carry out most tasks such as browsing the Web, watching movies, word processing, ordering food, coding, and so forth—being something that might be considered useful in a mobile setting to mobile computing being the expectation. With this expectation of computing and working from anywhere, the Web design and development community needed a new model for building a Web that could support an emerging mobile platform and a growing number of devices and operating systems. We found that model in the phrase "responsive Web design," also referenced by the acronym "RWD." Ethan Marcotte introduced the phrase and foundational RWD model in his List Apart article "Responsive Web Design" in May 2010 and followed with a book, *Responsive Web Design*, to further define and explicate the method. What is interesting about the passage of these five years is how far RWD has come from a fascinating, groundbreaking way of thinking about Web design and development to the industry standard today.

At its core, RWD is a set of techniques for building Web sites that work on multiple devices and screens. It allows content to flex and layout to change based on the size and capabilities of the device and screen.

When coming up with the idea, Marcotte took his inspiration from the emerging field of "responsive architecture," which considered how physical spaces adapt and respond to the presence of people passing through them. Building on this idea of responsiveness and HTML content passing through many screens and devices, Marcotte introduced the core concepts of RWD including:

- Fluid Grid Layouts—constructing HTML to be modular and adaptable to screen size.
- Flexible Objects—optimizing images, audio, videos, and so on to adjust to their containing elements as screen sizes change.
- Media Queries—applying the CSS media query to watch for screen and content breakpoints that allow pages to have specific styles tailored for the current display.

Placing the idea of flexible content first liberated our conception of the Web as a fixed medium, and a new way of designing and developing for the Web emerged.

1.2 WHY DO I NEED TO LEARN RWD (AND READ THIS BOOK)?

I love history and it is good to have in mind the broader picture of how we got here, but this book is primarily a practical guide. In this book, I focus on the whys and hows of RWD. The core of the book is an implementation chapter (chapter 5) that follows a cookbook model where readers can download the RWD code project and build it following a code walk-through. My goal was to make sure readers had a chance to learn and do. RWD is a fun enterprise and seeing the code in action can deliver a number of "aha!" moments; this book should provide those opportunities. Other chapters provide background on the conceptual model of RWD (chapter 2) and look forward to what's next for RWD (chapter 7). Some chapters are more reference based and I work through and discuss the current tools, frameworks resources, and tips and tricks for applying RWD (chapters 3, 6, and 8). And finally, we get to hear from a number of library practitioners speaking about their approaches to RWD and how they have changed their design and development practices in the case studies in chapter 4.

But even beyond the book content itself, there are some compelling reasons to learn RWD. I'll pick out some of the top reasons here. First on the list is the proliferation of operating systems and devices. Think about our contemporary computing environment—desktops, laptops, large-screen televisions, gaming consoles, tablets, notebooks, e-readers, and smartphones—each utilizing its own browser, screen resolutions, orientations, and layouts. In applying the RWD model, we can build once and let our content flow and respond to these various environments. Second, it saves money—money that otherwise might be spent for development of a site that works on specific devices and one that works on a desktop. A single RWD site is the cheaper option (most of the time). Third, RWD helps with search engine optimization (SEO) and machine readability of your content. Because RWD utilizes a consistent URL for each page, any site you design has uniform structure for desktop and mobile users and a consistent crawl pattern for search indexing bots. This improves user interaction, makes it easier for Google's link algorithms, and increases crawler efficiency. There are even new ranking metrics emerging within search engines that favor sites optimized to work across platforms using RWD principles (https://developers.google.com/webmasters/mobile-sites/mobile-seo/configurations/responsive-design). And finally, RWD asks you to think long and hard about performance and necessary content. This makes for a better user experience and a Web site centered around core actions. When you start to scale your design into small screens, the necessity of an extra link or an extra word to describe an action starts to matter. RWD creates restrictions, and this can be liberating, as a site is distilled to its essence. Cleaner designs and less code are the result.

1.3 WHAT PROBLEM IS RWD TRYING TO SOLVE?

RWD is starting to address the question of what it means to build for the Web in the age of mobile computing. And it is in its early stages. We are already seeing innovations in the RWD model, in the way that Web browsers process and serve content, and even in changes to the HTML specification itself to accommodate our multiple device and screen reality. As we work through the book together, we walk through what it means to apply a design solution to the problem of ubiquitous computing. We make things and break things and learn how RWD is evolving. Let's get started with RWD in practice.

2

GETTING STARTED

Responsive Web Design (RWD) in Practice

2.1 RWD CORE PRINCIPLES AND FUNCTIONALITY

In the interest of keeping things moving, I continue by looking at the core principles and techniques of RWD. I have outlined these techniques in the introduction, but there's more room here to explore what they are and how, as a whole, they form the complete RWD model. The goal of this chapter is to actually define the techniques and then show you how to apply them. There is code, or at least HTML and CSS. I close the chapter with a discussion of first considerations to take into account as you begin an RWD project.

We haven't actually seen how RWD works, and it is probably time to give a demonstration. This is where the printed word fails a bit, and I wish I could embed an animated .gif that shows the process of resizing a browser viewport. One of the best demonstrations of RWD concepts is a series of animated .gifs from the folks at the Froont Open Design Blog (http://blog.froont.com/9-basic-principles-of-responsive-web-design/). Feel free to go look at it now. I'll be here. When you are back, here's a series of screenshots of one of the apps we will build in chapter 5 showing the different display states for an RWD Web site. We are going to start small and scale up in following a "mobile first" approach, so figure 2.1 is our small-screen view that might work well with phone devices.

Note how the typography is optimized to fit within a smaller reading pane. You can also see that the navigation is pulled out of view and connected to a "menu" button action that slides the navigation into view when the user requests or touches it. The second screenshot shows another display option more oriented toward a tablet or e-reader view.

Here you can see the text start to stretch out and the line height move for maximum readability. This view is the sweet spot for a reader of the content on this Web site. The menu button is still in place and the navigation remains compressed and out of the way. Our third view is a large-screen design that should look familiar. This is the view that we would see on our desktop or laptop displays.

With the extra screen real estate, you can see the design starts to stretch out. The navigation is now a global header with a full title. Breadcrumb links are in place. A second column flows into view on the

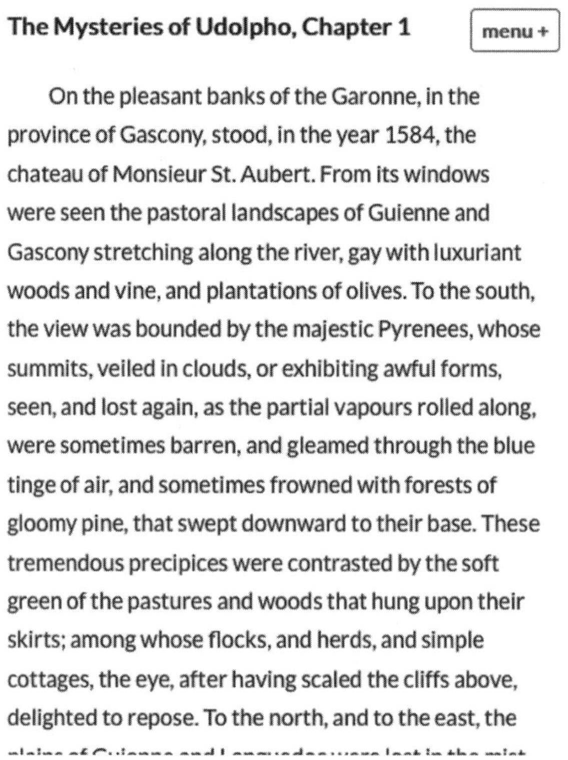

The Mysteries of Udolpho, Chapter 1   menu +

On the pleasant banks of the Garonne, in the province of Gascony, stood, in the year 1584, the chateau of Monsieur St. Aubert. From its windows were seen the pastoral landscapes of Guienne and Gascony stretching along the river, gay with luxuriant woods and vine, and plantations of olives. To the south, the view was bounded by the majestic Pyrenees, whose summits, veiled in clouds, or exhibiting awful forms, seen, and lost again, as the partial vapours rolled along, were sometimes barren, and gleamed through the blue tinge of air, and sometimes frowned with forests of gloomy pine, that swept downward to their base. These tremendous precipices were contrasted by the soft green of the pastures and woods that hung upon their skirts; among whose flocks, and herds, and simple cottages, the eye, after having scaled the cliffs above, delighted to repose. To the north, and to the east, the

Figure 2.1.   Web Bookreader Interface on Small Screen

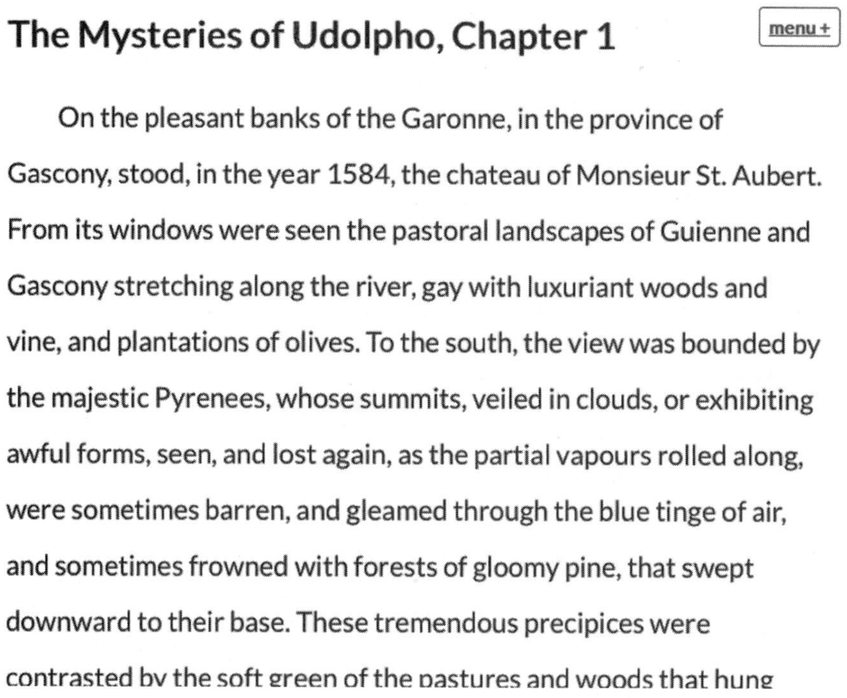

The Mysteries of Udolpho, Chapter 1 [menu +]

On the pleasant banks of the Garonne, in the province of Gascony, stood, in the year 1584, the chateau of Monsieur St. Aubert. From its windows were seen the pastoral landscapes of Guienne and Gascony stretching along the river, gay with luxuriant woods and vine, and plantations of olives. To the south, the view was bounded by the majestic Pyrenees, whose summits, veiled in clouds, or exhibiting awful forms, seen, and lost again, as the partial vapours rolled along, were sometimes barren, and gleamed through the blue tinge of air, and sometimes frowned with forests of gloomy pine, that swept downward to their base. These tremendous precipices were contrasted by the soft green of the pastures and woods that hung

Figure 2.2. Web Bookreader Interface on Intermediate Screen

left holding metadata. The real benefit here is that the whole design view trajectory and movement between screens captured in the screenshots above is based on one HTML foundation set up to flow between small, medium, and large views. RWD gives us this capability, and in the next part of this chapter, I unpack the components that make up this design model: fluid grid layouts, flexible objects, and media queries.

Fluid Grid Layouts

The first key component of RWD is the application of a fluid grid for layout. The fluid grid is not a single technology, but a principle for setting the width and size of HTML elements on a Web page with relative units. The concept to keep in mind here is how we might set widths in percentages versus pixels. When people first started building Web pages, we brought what I would call a print mind-set into our

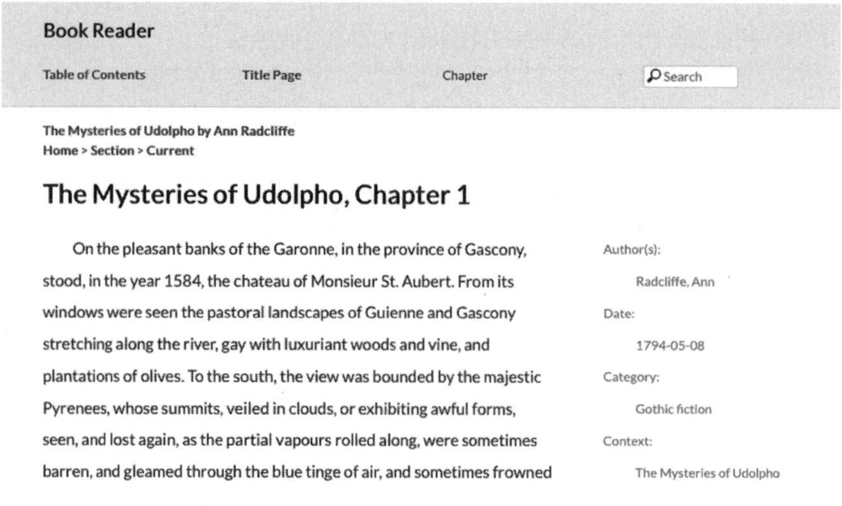

Book Reader

Table of Contents   Title Page   Chapter   🔍 Search

The Mysteries of Udolpho by Ann Radcliffe
Home > Section > Current

The Mysteries of Udolpho, Chapter 1

On the pleasant banks of the Garonne, in the province of Gascony, stood, in the year 1584, the chateau of Monsieur St. Aubert. From its windows were seen the pastoral landscapes of Guienne and Gascony stretching along the river, gay with luxuriant woods and vine, and plantations of olives. To the south, the view was bounded by the majestic Pyrenees, whose summits, veiled in clouds, or exhibiting awful forms, seen, and lost again, as the partial vapours rolled along, were sometimes barren, and gleamed through the blue tinge of air, and sometimes frowned

Author(s):
Radcliffe, Ann
Date:
1794-05-08
Category:
Gothic fiction
Context:
The Mysteries of Udolpho

Figure 2.3.   Web Bookreader Interface on Large Screen

designs. Print design worked within constraints such as paper size, bindings, and margins. With this metaphor in mind, we built fixed-width pages that worked within certain screen sizes. Let me unpack this idea a little bit with a counter-example using HTML and CSS. The markup for a typical HTML page with a <main> container and two <section> tags broken into two columns might look something like this source code.

```
<!doctype html>
<html lang="en">
<head>
<meta charset="utf-8">
<meta name="viewport" content="width=device-width,initial-scale=1">
<title>RWD in Practice - Grid/Column Example</title>
<link rel="stylesheet" href="style.css">
</head>
<body>
<main class="container">
<section class="primary">
</section>
<section class="secondary">
</section>
```

```
</main>
</body>
</html>
```

The fixed-width set of styles to make this markup appear as a two-column layout with the primary column taking up two-thirds of the page would appear as the lines below in a CSS stylesheet (the style.css file in the <link> tag above).

```
/* Fixed-width two columns */
.container {
width:1024px;margin:0 auto;padding:0;
}
.primary {
float:left;width:680px;margin:0;padding:0;
}
.secondary {
float:left;width:340px;margin:0;padding:0;
}
```

Here's the question: how can this design scale into a screen that is larger or smaller than 1,024 pixels? The answer is that it can't really. On larger screens, it will appear in the middle of the browser with large margins on the right and left. On smaller screens, it is much worse, as the content maintains its large width and some of the columns push off the screen viewport, keeping it from a user's view. Two techniques come into play here to make a flexible layout possible. First, we add a new <meta> tag in the <head> of our document that tells the browser to monitor and respond to the width of the virtual viewport of the device.

```
<meta name="viewport" content="width=device-width,initial-scale=1">
```

The <meta name="viewport"> with the width=device-width attribute forces the browser to work with the actual, current size of the screen, and that allows us to have a baseline for the relative unit measurements we will apply to our grids and columns. For more background on the <meta name="viewport"> tag, the Mozilla Developer network has a solid article on how it works in mobile settings (https://developer.mozilla.org/en-US/docs/Mozilla/Mobile/Viewport_meta_tag). So, picking back up with our idea of fluidity and relative units, we can apply our second technique and make a simple change to our CSS rules to start building using the fluid grid/column component of RWD. The revised CSS file is below.

```
/* Fluid-width two columns */
.container {
width:100%;margin:0 auto;
}
.primary {
float:left;width:65%;margin:0;padding:0;
}
.secondary {
float:left;width:33%;margin:0;padding:0;
}
```

Note the switch in declaring the width of each HTML division. It's not much of a change, but the difference is drastic. Our columns now flow and adjust to any screen size, keeping the two-third to one-third ratio and all content remains visible. In assigning percentage widths to the <main> container as well as the primary and secondary <section>s, we have put in place the fluid grid principle. And there are new ways of creating grids and columns, besides the old-school float, coming forward. (See the CSS grid property, https://css-tricks.com/snippets/css/complete-guide-grid/, and CSS flexible boxes, https://developer.mozilla.org/en-US/docs/Web/Guide/CSS/Flexible_boxes, for a peek at how we'll build columns and grids in the future.) The key to the fluid grid component of RWD is finding relative units for HTML layout elements that can respond to changes in screen size and display requirements. Percentages are one way to apply relative units, but there are others like em, rem, and points, which work by staying relative to base font sizes or root elements of the HTML document (https://css-tricks.com/the-lengths-of-css/).

Flexible Objects (Images, Audio, Video, Etc.)

Another related problem that developers address in RWD is how to make media objects fluid and "flowable." Because browsers usually require a width declaration for video and image elements, these elements are commonly displayed as fixed width. As we saw, layouts break when we have fixed-width elements and we have to move between screens and devices. RWD developers follow a similar development pattern of introducing fluidity to these static objects. First, we make sure the <meta name="viewport"> tag in the <head> of our document has another attribute that tells the browser not to perform an initial zoom when visiting the page.

<meta name="viewport" content="width=device-width,initial-scale=1">

The <meta name="viewport"> with the initial-scale=1 attribute prevents an image (or media object) from scaling up to its original size and breaking our layout. The second technique is to apply the max-width CSS rule coupled with the width CSS rule using relative units. A CSS rule set example is below for a flexible image.

img {width:100%;max-width:100%;height:auto;}

The initial width rule helps older browsers display the image responsively. We use the cascading inheritance of CSS to let browsers that understand max-width pick up the second rule. And finally, we add a height:auto rule to help browser performance, as the browser looks for both height and width as it tries to render media objects. The end result of this series of rules is that the maximum width of the image is set to 100 percent of the screen or browser width, so when that 100 percent becomes smaller, the image (or media object) follows suit. This fluid CSS rule pattern should start to look familiar. The idea for these static and fixed media objects is to assign relative units that allow them to shift into new sizes. The width, max-width, height:auto pattern works on a majority of static media objects, and you can follow the pattern with most of your <video> and <audio> objects, or any object that you want to make flexible. However, there are some exceptions and enhancements worth considering. One of these exceptions is what to do with media content that we embed from other sites. Take for example the common practice of placing a YouTube video and its associated video player on your page. This embed code is usually an <iframe> with a fixed width. How do we control and turn external content into responsive content? The answer is to control the HTML element where you are going to embed external content. Let's walk through a simple example of a You-

Tube embed. First, we build an HTML container that we can style responsively.

```
<section class="responsive-container">
<iframe src="http://youtube.com/embed/m4cgLL8JaVl?rel=0" frameborder
="0" allowfullscreen>
</iframe>
</section>
```

Second, we apply some CSS rules that tell the content how to work within the screen size that is available.

```
.responsive-container {
position:relative;padding-bottom:56.25%;padding-top:30px;height:  0;over-
flow: hidden;
}
.responsive-container  iframe  {position:absolute;top:  0;left:0;width:100%;
height:100%;
}
```

The CSS rules above use an approach that places an absolutely positioned element inside a relative one. The trick here is making sure to assign relative units to the embedded content (in this case, the <iframe>). There is also a relative unit on the padding bottom that creates an intrinsic ratio for the embedded content, which allows browsers to determine embedded content dimensions based on the width of its containing block (in this case, our <section class="responsive-container">). See Thierry Koblentz's article "Creating Intrinsic Ratios for Video" for a complete discussion of the technique (http://alista-part.com/article/creating-intrinsic-ratios-for-video). Taking a step back, this pattern of absolutely positioning an element inside of a relative container and using relative units to size the content is another means of building flexible objects. For example, you could work through a similar set of rules and markup for embedding a flexible Google map. Flexible objects are easily one of the more complex components of RWD, but these techniques can get you started and provide a working model for implementation of this important facet of RWD.

CSS Media Queries

CSS media queries are the special sauce of RWD (https://developer.mozilla.org/en-US/docs/Web/Guide/CSS/Media_queries). They are the piece that enables our designs to flow between displays by monitoring and reacting to the current screen size and all kinds of device variables. From a more technical point of view, a media query watches for a specific condition (in most cases, screen size), and when that condition is true, a certain set of style rules or a completely new stylesheet is applied, following the normal cascading rules. The media query syntax looks pretty straightforward, but there is a whole lot of complexity and learning to do once you start to understand the syntax. There are two primary ways to call and encode a media query. First, you can follow the embedded media query method like the example below. Imagine you are declaring the rules below inside of a stylesheet.

```
body {
background:gray;
}
<!-- CSS media query embedded within a stylesheet -->
@media all and (max-width:600px) {
.facet_sidebar {display:none;}
}
```

The second way is to follow the external media query method by extending the existing media part of the link element or @import rule. In this case, you would be modifying the HTML markup in the <head> of the document.

```
<link href="small.css" rel="stylesheet" media="all and (max-width:
600px)">
```

The media query syntax itself works within three declarations. The first declaration is an **@media** rule (https://developer.mozilla.org/en-US/docs/Web/CSS/@media) to designate the beginning of a media query expression. The second declaration is the media type (https://developer.mozilla.org/en-US/docs/Web/CSS/@media#Media_types) that assigns the device type to apply the query to some predefined type or output (e.g., **screen, print, all,** etc.). The third declaration is the logical test and expression for media features (https://developer.mozilla.org/

en-US/docs/Web/CSS/@media#Media_features). Of the three, media features are the most complex, as they give us all kinds of options to check for and test against. I won't go into all of the details here, but the farther down the media feature rabbit hole you go, the more you can test for some really interesting conditions. You can even start watching for screen resolution orientation and introduce logical conditions like not and only.

```
@media only screen
and (min-width:768px)
and (max-width:1024px)
and (orientation:landscape)
and (min-resolution:200dpi)
{ /* styles that meet the conditions for a retina display iPad here */ }
```

There is potential for structuring and tuning your Web pages to work exclusively for certain devices and conditions. Like I said, the media query is the special sauce. With a wide variety of rules and options, we can transform our Web pages based on context. This is powerful magic. As for best practices in declaring your media queries, I start with the embedded media query method because I like to avoid the conditional or extra loading of CSS files of the external media query method, which can impact performance based on the extra HTTP request the browser has to make for the file. It also helps me to keep a handle on all the different conditions I am using for the media queries when I have them lined up in the same file.

A final consideration of your media queries is to determine what we call "breakpoints" for your content. Breakpoints are the places at which you make a decision to flow content into a different view layout or screen dimension. In the beginning of RWD, we tended to assign breakpoints based on known device dimensions, but as devices proliferated, the fixed nature of these media queries didn't always work. A best practice in RWD these days is to think of your content on small, medium, and large screens. I should note that what constitutes small, medium, and large depends on your project. The best way to test where your breakpoints might be is to load your pages or a prototype page and resize the browser window. Let's go back to our earlier Web bookreader example to get a picture of this process. Below you see that I have resized the browser window to around 804 pixels.

At this point, you can start to see the default, large-screen view start to break down. The body text does not have enough characters for a comfortable readability level. The global navigation is getting crowded. The left column is now too narrow. Once you see this kind of downgrade in look and feel, you know that you have a potential breakpoint. In the CSS for the Web Bookreader example, I assigned a breakpoint at around 800 pixels using the following media query rule.

```
/*medium screen view < 801px (based on 16px default)*/
@media all and (max-width:50.1em) {
/* styles that meet medium screen conditions here */
}
```

It is dependent on your own content and perception, but building breakpoints following this content flow and browser resize method will serve you well in most cases. For further reading on some best practices and cutting-edge cases around media queries, see Brad Frost's "7 Hab-

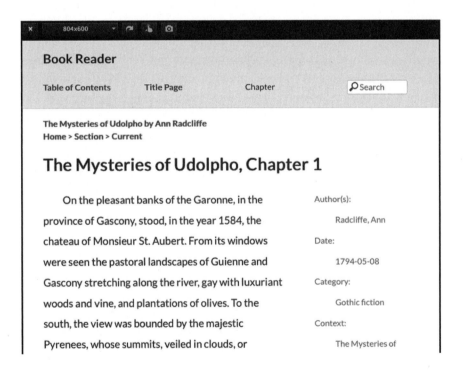

Figure 2.4.   Web Bookreader Interface at 804 Pixels

its of Highly Effective Media Queries" (http://bradfrost.com/blog/post/
7-habits-of-highly-effective-media-queries/).

Optimization and Performance

I hinted at performance earlier when discussing setting a height on our
flexible objects. In that instance, the goal was to reduce the burden on
the browser to do some guesswork around the height of an image. It
may seem small, but these types of page overheads can add up. RWD is
a great model, but one of its drawbacks is the hidden page weights of
extensive, expansive CSS files, large HTML files with markup that is
only used in certain screen views, and even JavaScript and edge techniques that push browser-rendering engines to their limits. With these
potential bottlenecks, performance and optimization is a first-class concern for RWD Web sites. Fortunately, there are emerging techniques
for addressing some of these concerns.

A first technique related to performance and optimization is minimizing http requests. The fastest HTML element, CSS rule, or external
file is the one that is never called (or doesn't exist). When building or
auditing your responsive design, the first place to start is looking at
whether a file needs to be linked and brought onto the page. The more
requests a browser has to make for an external file, the slower things
can get. It becomes an even bigger concern on mobile edge networks. If
you're not careful, you could be pushing files that are only needed for
larger screens down to a smartphone. A couple of techniques to help
with this are inlining your CSS, setting your scripts to load asynchronously (and at the bottom of the page), and taking advantage of content
delivery networks. Turning your CSS into a set of inline styles means
adding the CSS rules directly into the <head> of the HTML page. In
this scenario, the external <link> reference would be removed.

```
<!doctype html>
<html lang="en">
<head>
<meta charset="utf-8">
<meta name="viewport" content="width=device-width,initial-scale=1">
<title>RWD in Practice - Grid/Column Example</title>
<link rel="stylesheet" href="style.css">
</head>
```

```
<body>
<main class="container">
<section class="primary">
</section>
<section class="secondary">
</section>
</main>
</body>
</html>
```

In turn, the styles would be embedded on the page directly using <style> tags.

```
<!doctype html>
<html lang="en">
<head>
<meta charset="utf-8">
<meta name="viewport" content="width=device-width,initial-scale=1">
<title>RWD in Practice - Grid/Column Example</title>
<style>
html   {background:#eff1f3;-webkit-font-smoothing:antialiased;-moz-osx-fo
nt-smoothing:grayscale;overflow-y:scroll;-webkit-text-size-adjust:100%;-
ms-text-size-adjust:100%;}
html,body {width:100%;height:100%;margin:0;padding:0;}
body   {background:#fff;color:#000;font-family:Lato,"Helvetica   Neue",Arial,
Helvetica,sans-serif;font-size:100%;line-height:1.5;}
a {font-weight:700;text-decoration:none;}
a:link,a:visited {color:#369;}
a:hover,a:focus,a:active {outline:0;text-decoration:underline;}
h1,h2,h3,ol,ul,dl,p {margin-top:0;margin-bottom:1.5rem;max-width:45em;}
img     {border:0;-ms-interpolation-mode:bicubic;height:auto;max-width:100
%;}
...
ALL the rest of the styles here
...
</style>
</head>
<body>
<main class="container">
<section class="primary">
</section>
```

```
<section class="secondary">
</section>
</main>
</body>
</html>
```

The main advantage is that there is no longer a second file to call onto the page. The browser makes one request and has the HTML and CSS. This technique works well for smaller, concentrated stylesheets, but breaks down a bit if you are bringing in a stylesheet with thousands of lines. A corollary to this first optimization technique is to be judicious with your HTML markup and CSS style rules. Do you really need the extra <div> to wrap an element, or could you reuse an HTML element already on the page? Is that style on the single <p> tag necessary, or could it be inherited from an earlier style rule? Keeping this efficient mind-set is a key component of "mobile first" RWD thinking and a Web site that performs well. Being smart about how, when, and where to load your scripts is another component of minimizing the overhead of HTTP requests. Placing scripts near the end of the <body> of your page, you are giving priority of your HTTP request to those files and rules that provide the visual rendering of a page. This makes for a page that appears and loads faster. Here's another example from our stock HTML page we have been using in this chapter.

```
<!doctype html>
<html lang="en">
<head>
<meta charset="utf-8">
<meta name="viewport" content="width=device-width,initial-scale=1">
<title>RWD in Practice - Grid/Column Example</title>
<link rel="stylesheet" href="style.css">
</head>
<body>
<main class="container">
<section class="primary">
</section>
<section class="secondary">
</section>
</main>
<script async src="/scripts/main.js"<</script>
```

```
</body>
</html>
```

The script appears at the end of the document and doesn't block the loading of the HTML and CSS that we are using to build the visual display. We have also tagged the script with an async attribute that tells the browser to load the script asynchronously. That is, we are telling the browser not to stop what it's doing while it's downloading this script. Browsers have a limited number of requests and threads that they can carry out at one time, and the asynchronous declaration helps them prioritize. A final component of our minimizing HTTP request efforts is to consider using a content delivery network (CDN). A CDN is a network that improves performance by caching static content such as images, CSS, JavaScript, videos, and so on for a Web site on servers distributed around the world. This helps improve the load time of a Web site by loading the static content from the closest CDN server. Your mileage may vary if your site is small and primarily has local Internet traffic, but some CDNs can be a good investment. You could place or load any common (especially large) files that you wanted within the network and build your site with links referencing the location of your files in the CDN. Some free CDN options include BootstrapCDN (www.bootstrapcdn.com/) and CloudFlareYou (www.cloudflare.com/features-cdn). There are also pay CDN options like Amazon Cloud-Front (http://aws.amazon.com/cloudfront/).

A second technique related to RWD performance and optimization is minification. Minification is a technique that focuses on compressing files by removing unnecessary or redundant data without impacting how the file is processed and understood by a Web browser. In the case of HTML, CSS, or JavaScript files, this means removing extra white space, code comments, formatting, applying shorthand variable and function names. If this sounds like a lot, it is. But there are tools online that can do the minification for you. Let me show what this looks like in practice. Here's our unminified HTML from earlier.

```
<!doctype html>
<html lang="en">
<head>
<meta charset="utf-8">
<meta name="viewport" content="width=device-width,initial-scale=1">
```

```
<title>RWD in Practice - Grid/Column Example</title>
<link rel="stylesheet" href="style.css">
</head>
<body>
<main class="container">
<section class="primary">
</section>
<section class="secondary">
</section>
</main>
<script async src="/scripts/main.js"></script>
</body>
</html>
```

After minification, the same file looks like the example file below.

```
<!doctype html><html lang="en"><head><meta charset="utf-8">
<meta name="viewport" content="width=device-width,initial-scale=1">
<title>RWD in Practice - Grid/Column Example</title><link
rel="stylesheet" href="style.css"></head><body><main
class="container"><section class="primary"></section><section
class="secondary"></section></main><script async src="/scripts/
main.js"></script></body></html>
```

The idea is to compress the file so that it can still be understood by the
browser while reducing the size to allow for a faster load. Many good
text editors display the file so that it is human-readable and then keep
the compression when you save it. Again, your mileage will vary, but on
larger, complex CSS files, minification can boost performance. I mentioned minification tools earlier and here are a few to look at as you get
started: HTML Minifier (www.willpeavy.com/minifier/), CSS Minifier
(http://cssminifier.com), JavaScript Minifier (http://javascript-minifi-
er.com), and Dirty Markup (www.dirtymarkup.com/).

A third technique related to performance and optimization is compressing media objects and serving images correctly. Recent studies
have shown that average Web page weights continue to grow and have
reached "1,953Kb—a little under 2Mb—and are comprised of 95 indi-
vidual HTTP requests" as of December 2014 (www.sitepoint.com/aver-
age-page-weight-increases-15-2014/). With the emphasis on a single
HTML file and large CSS for complex media queries, RWD might be

one reason. A more likely explanation, however, is our expectation as developers that networks are always on, that they have plenty of bandwidth, and that our images have not been compressed. From that Site-Point article I just mentioned, the largest files on the page were the images coming in at 1,243 kilobytes out of the 1,953 kilobytes of the total Web page size. This speaks to our need to be smart about how we load media objects—specifically images—into our pages. A first step is to optimize and compress images correctly. There are a number of stand-alone utilities like FileOptimizer (http://nikkhokkho.sourceforge .net/static.php?page=FileOptimizer), OptiPNG (http://optipng .sourceforge.net/), and ImageOptim (https://imageoptim.com/) that can help you get your files in order. Alternatively, online tools such as Smush.it (http://www.smushit.com/ysmush.it/) or TinyPNG (https://ti-nypng.com/) can do the work in the cloud. Once you have your media files compressed and optimized, a next step is to use some of the emerging responsive image techniques to serve image files. One of the most promising is the <img> srcset attribute. An example follows.

```
<img src="./your-logo-sm.png"
srcset="./your-logo-sm.png 320w,
./your-logo-med.png 720w,
./your-logo-lrg.png 1024w"
alt="@my Library"/>
```

The srcset attribute allows you to add some logic to a standard <img> tag to watch for different screen dimensions and to match the image width declared at the end of each image link. So the 720w image would match large smartphones and tablets and get served to those devices. Another benefit to this approach is that browsers that don't support srcset will use the img src= to present an image. It's backward compatible. There are other emerging standards for RWD media like the <picture> element, but they aren't quite ready for implementation without JavaScript polyfills (extra JavaScript helper scripts that educate browsers on how to use an element). That said, there are means to present media objects intelligently and as you start to work within RWD, it will benefit you to know about and implement these practices. Your users will thank you.

2.2 HOW TO START CREATING YOUR OWN RESPONSIVE WEB DESIGNS

With a discussion of the foundations of RWD in place, it's time to start talking about how to evaluate a project for RWD and about the things to think about as you get started with the RWD model. This evaluation checklist will help you get your head around the needs and shape of an RWD project.

Does your Web site need an RWD treatment?

This is a great first question. RWD is an important design and development trend, but if your site is a single page listing your hours, contact information, and a link to your catalog, you might not need the complexity of RWD.

Are you prepared to "get under the hood" on your new RWD site more than your traditional site, since it requires more time and skills with HTML, CSS, and JavaScript?

Over the course of this chapter, you got a picture of the complexity behind RWD. I'm not mentioning this complexity to scare you away, but it is worth considering how much time it might take for you to feel comfortable working with RWD. Do you have time within your position to do this (especially if you are getting started with RWD)? Talk with your supervisor or your employees about the increased need for resources involved in RWD.

Are you okay with the design limitations of RWD?

With an emphasis on "mobile first," the small screen is where you start with RWD. Does your library site work on the small screen? It may be that your site is too complex to work inside of an RWD model. You may also have other parties within the organization who need complexity and details that you won't be able to accommodate in the RWD design model. I'm thinking here about your outreach and branding units. Do they understand what RWD might mean for their work?

Do I have metrics to show a need for an RWD?

This one is really essential. Take a look at your analytics package and check your mobile and operating systems visits. Are Android or iOS in the top ten for operating system statistics? You want your decision to move into RWD to have a data point or two.

Do you have target mobile and tablet devices in mind?

Related to the analysis of your Web metrics and statistics, start to sketch out your targets for small, medium, and large screens. It will help as you strategize about your RWD breakpoints during development. It will also help stakeholders start to understand how RWD reaches a broad audience and multiple devices.

Exactly how will an RWD increase traffic to the site, if at all?

Have a plan for what a successful site looks like. Are you expecting increased mobile visits to the catalog? Write down the expectations and goals and make sure you can assess whether those expectations and goals have been achieved.

After reading this chapter, you have an RWD evaluation in hand and a solid understanding of the RWD model. It's time to start thinking about implementation and turn toward the frameworks and tools that can help you build an RWD Web site in chapter 3.

3

TOOLS AND APPLICATIONS

Responsive Web Design (RWD) in Practice

3.1 THE RAPID GROWTH OF RWD TOOLS, FRAMEWORKS, AND PROCESSES

Even as RWD is in its infancy (remember, it is barely five years old), the number of tools and resources related to learning and automating the tasks of RWD are growing and emerging at such a pace that it is hard to keep up. The rapid growth of RWD tools and resources speaks to how essential the RWD model has become for modern Web development. It also speaks to the complexity of the model and how tools and frameworks are needed to support RWD implementation. In this chapter, we look to staying in front of RWD and learning about the important tools, frameworks, and processes that help us as make our sites responsive. I follow a format of defining the generic concept of the tool and then explaining or annotating a number of specific tools so that we can all get a sense of how to use them. The goal is to provide background and insight into why you might choose a particular tool in addition to explaining how you might get started using it.

3.2 RWD FRAMEWORKS

The first set of tools is the RWD frameworks. In this context, a framework is a collection of files—scripts, HTML, CSS, and so forth—that give developers a head start in building a Web application. RWD frameworks have files that produce the look and feel, navigation, breakpoints, cross-browser tested CSS rules, and much more. They are great options for prototyping and for organizations with smaller teams, since they allow you to get an RWD site up and running in a short amount of time. In essence, RWD frameworks give you a prebuilt site and your work is in learning the rules of the framework and customizing it for your own needs.

Bootstrap

Bootstrap (http://getbootstrap.com/) is the most popular of the three frameworks we will review. It evolved from Twitter's Web development process when two Twitter software engineers released their code on github.com. It is widely tested across platforms and screens, simple to implement, follows a "mobile first" design strategy, works within a grid design pattern, and has a huge community of support and documentation. To get started, you download the collection of files and post them to your Web server space. Bootstrap has some critics who argue that the framework's success has led to too many Web sites looking exactly the same, but you can't deny that it works and has a whole suite of tools and documentation to get an RWD site up in a short amount of time.

Foundation ZURB

Foundation ZURB (Foundation for short; http://foundation.zurb.com/) is another popular framework. Like Bootstrap, it has a strong developer community and great documentation. Foundation has a series of starter templates that are easy to use and get you a quick RWD prototype in moments. It is widely tested across platforms and screens, follows a grid design pattern, and is flexible in that it is more style agnostic than Bootstrap (you can customize the look and feel more easily). Foundation also has a strong training and support section to help you as you learn the framework. It also has strong integration with other development tools like SASS (a CSS processing tool). If anything, Foundation might have drawbacks regarding its flexibility, as it gives you many choices for design. Others argue that this is a strength and its best feature.

Skeleton

Skeleton (http://getskeleton.com/) is the leanest of the frameworks mentioned here and primarily an HTML and CSS template. One drawback of both Bootstrap and Foundation is that they come packaged with a number of files—some of which you may never use—which leads to a lot of bloat and wasted space. Skeleton takes a less-is-more approach to the framework idea. It's a good fit if you're embarking on a smaller project or if you don't feel like you need the utility of larger frameworks. Skeleton is built using a handful of standard HTML elements and includes a grid layout. It gives you the most control of the three frameworks mentioned, but it has less documentation, mostly due to its simplicity.

3.3 RWD IN CONTENT MANAGEMENT SYSTEMS (CMS): PLUGINS AND TECHNIQUES

Many of us work with content management systems (CMS), which have allowed our organizations to enable content creators and build our Web sites quickly. CMSs are widely implemented and give us the chance to use a database to store all of our Web site content. We also gain a steady set of templates for design that can help ease site development. A drawback of the CMS is that we have to work within the CSS, HTML, and scripting languages that make up the CMS software. Fortunately, there are development processes and plugins—bits of prebuilt software that hook into the CMS—that we can use to customize the CMS or add new features. In this section, I review some RWD plugins and techniques to give you a sense of how you might apply RWD to a CMS. My focus is on Drupal (www.drupal.org/) and WordPress (wordpress.org/), as these CMSs are widely implemented in libraries and cultural organizations.

Bones (WordPress)

The first resource is Bones (http://themble.com/bones/), a mobile-first, responsive theme for WordPress. It boasts a strong and active line of development in its github repository (https://github.com/eddiemacha-do/bones), which is something you want to look for in choosing any plugin or theme. If it hasn't had active development in years, that is a bad sign. Bones is a free theme that strips much of the WordPress template down to its core. It uses modern Web standards borrowed from the HTML5 Boilerplate (https://html5boilerplate.com/) and includes good documentation for getting set up.

AdaptiveTheme (Drupal)

AdaptiveTheme (www.drupal.org/project/adaptivetheme) is a Drupal theme framework with an emphasis on responsive design. It even allows you to set up specific layouts for different device groups, such as desktop, tablet, and smartphone, all via the user interface and without any coding. The documentation (http://adaptivethemes.com/documenta-tion) is extensive and it has an active record of development showing recent commits to the source code.

Creating Mobile-Optimized Web Sites Using WordPress

For those interested in learning how a WordPress CMS can be mod-ified to work responsively, *Smashing Magazine*'s tutorial (www.smashingmagazine.com/2012/05/24/creating-mobile-optimized-websites-using-wordpress/) is a great place to start. It lists a number of themes and plugins to consider before moving into the actual work of how to define media queries for WordPress, making the layout respon-sive and modifying the global navigation for small screens.

Zen (Drupal)

Zen (www.drupal.org/project/zen) is another Drupal starter theme built around a responsive, mobile-first grid design as its default layout. It has great documentation (www.drupal.org/node/193318), including videos showing how to set it up. It also has a strong development history and commitment to Web accessibility, which is important for public institutions like libraries.

3.4 OPTIMIZATION AND PERFORMANCE

In chapter 2 I spoke about the need to think about optimization and performance of your RWD site, but I didn't have a chance to look closely at the tools that can help you optimize files and guide you toward best practices. In this section, I look at resources that can compress or minify files as well as tools that analyze your site and provide guidelines for improving page load times and other micro-optimizations.

Image Compression

Images remain the largest files within any Web page, but there are some tools that can compress the unnecessary bits from these files. I favor online image compressors for ease of use, but there are a number of stand-alone utilities like FileOptimizer (http://nikkhokk-ho.sourceforge.net/static.php?page=FileOptimizer), OptiPNG (http://optipng.sourceforge.net/), and ImageOptim (https://imageoptim.com/) that can help you get your files in order. As mentioned, I prefer the online variety and tools such as Smush.it (www.smushit.com/ysmush.it/) and TinyPNG (https://tinypng.com/), which can do the work in the cloud. Just submit a URL or upload your image and you'll get the compressed image as a download.

Minification Tools for HTML, CSS, and JavaScript

The act of compressing text files for delivery over the network is not a new practice, but it has risen in importance as RWD HTML, CSS, and JavaScript files have grown in size. Much like images, these files can contribute to slower load times and the sense that your site isn't responding quickly. The term "minification" is used to describe the process where extraneous characters, white space, and redundant code are removed to save space in text files. There are a number of minification tools available and some of my favorites are listed below.

- HTML Minifier (www.willpeavy.com/minifier/)
- CSS Minifier (http://cssminifier.com)
- JavaScript Minifier (http://javascript-minifier.com)
- Dirty Markup (www.dirtymarkup.com/)

Performance Tools

Speed matters. It's a simple statement, but it does apply to how well your RWD site is understood and trusted. A site with a fast loading time and one that works quickly as you change states within your pages is generally understood to be a good design. Testing performance and being able to understand the messages these tools give you is an important skill to develop. My favorite performance tool is Google PageSpeed (https://developers.google.com/speed/pagespeed/). PageSpeed exists as an online tool and as a browser extension. Simply load your site URL, run the test, and PageSpeed gives you a performance grade along with high (red), medium (yellow), pass (green) grades for features of your site along with the tips for how to improve. GTmetrix (http://gtmetrix.com/) is an online port of Yahoo's YSlow analysis tool with rich performance reports with even more detail than PageSpeed. I also like YellowLab Tools' (http://yellowlab.tools/) online performance test as it includes an audit of how you might fix your HTML and JavaScript. When I design, I use a combination of each of these tools to get a broad picture of performance. It is worth running tests in multiple tools as you can find new issues within different tools that measure different emphases.

3.5 PREVIEWING TOOLS AND EMULATORS

Previewing and testing your design across as many devices and screens as possible is a necessary component to RWD. A good place to start with testing is within your organization. Ask around to see if you can do live testing with staff willing to volunteer their devices. This helps, but you might miss some devices. It's at this point where emulators and previewing tools come in handy. My first place to start with emulators and previewing tools is within the Web browser. Both Chrome and Firefox have excellent RWD previewing tools. Firefox's Responsive Design View (https://developer.mozilla.org/en-US/docs/Tools/Respon-sive_Design_View) allows you to set custom breakpoints and flip orien-tation to test what happens to your design. Chrome DevTools also has a responsive design emulator that offers many of the same features but also includes some advanced testing using a list of common devices and a test for how your site might perform on slow or edge networks (https://developers.google.com/web/fundamentals/tools/devices/browseremu-lation). There are also some great online emulators each with a measur-ing grid and selections for just about every device you can imagine. Just submit your URL and you'll get to see your design in all types of set-tings. My two favorite online emulators are ScreenFly (http://quirk-tools.com/screenfly/) and Dimensions Toolkit (www.dimensionstoolkit.com/).

4

LIBRARY EXAMPLES AND CASE STUDIES
Responsive Web Design (RWD)

4.1 RWD WORKING IN LIBRARIES

In the relatively short time since the RWD model was introduced, it has become an industry standard and common practice for Web development. In many ways, RWD was inevitable, as it allows us to build from a single design and HTML foundation. It is a logical answer to the problem of multiple devices, new screen resolutions, and different screen sizes. This makes sense when you think of practices of efficiency and scale for Web development. But I would argue that this democratic development approach fits right into the goals of libraries and our interest in information access for all. That is, inherent to libraries is the need to not favor or design for particular platforms at the expense of access for all. RWD solves this problem by making sure library content and information is accessible via the largest installed app in existence, the Web browser. In this chapter, we consider possibilities for RWD in libraries and how specific libraries have embraced RWD in all types of their Web properties.

Common Applications for RWD in Libraries

Before we hear from actual library practitioners of RWD, I map out some of the most common and emerging-use case scenarios for RWD and library content. These RWD possibilities offer library developers a quick understanding of common design requirements for library content in the multiscreen world and demonstrate how libraries are beginning to apply the RWD model.

The Library Web site

The library Web site proper is one of the first places to start thinking about and building with RWD principles. Content that details library resources, staff, locations, and hours should be accessible on as many screens and platforms as possible. In many ways, RWD begins and ends with this common interface layer, and if you were to pursue RWD in only one place in your library, this is it. *Example: New York Public Library (www.nypl.org/).*

Content Designed for Mobile Devices

As RWD has become a viable design option, the idea of building a separate app or custom HTML Web site for mobile devices such as tablets or smartphones seems wasteful. Web apps built within the RWD model and optimized for mobile devices can provide the look and feel of a native application. The next time a library user asks about a library app and you consider your options, take a closer look at how RWD might solve that problem. *Example: JSTOR (www.jstor.org/).*

Information Kiosks and Promotional Displays

Large-screen displays with promotional announcements and messages are becoming more commonplace in libraries. Some libraries are even designing and incorporating interactive way-finding or instructional kiosks. These displays often require large screen and touch interface designs that are perfectly suited to media queries and the adaptive nature of the RWD model. *Example: My #HuntLibrary (http:// d.lib.ncsu.edu/myhuntlibrary).*

Wearable Computing and the Internet of Things

The idea of an Internet connected to everyday devices and the ability to wear a mobile computer is being promoted as a likely emerging technology. Smart thermostats and refrigerators, connected eyeglasses, and smart watches all have one thing in common: computer screens (and potentially a Web browser). Whether or not these products become a core consumer pattern remains to be seen, but the principles of RWD give us options for designing to reach these platforms. *Example: Apple Watch (www.apple.com/watch/overview/).*

Vendor Solutions

Library Web sites are often a composite of local HTML and purchased third-party products integrated into our overall design. The interaction patterns and design inconsistencies that occur as we try to stitch these systems together make for challenging user interfaces. A user can move from an elegantly designed library hours page that works seamlessly across platforms to a fixed-width library catalog search system that works best for a desktop computer. Reworking these systems using the product or vendor's application programming interface (API) is an option, and RWD is the best-practice approach for making that vendor catalog display work on multiple screens and platforms. *Example: Boise Public Library Catalog (www.boisepubliclibrary.org/mobile/).*

Case Studies and Commentary on RWD in Libraries

With our quick survey of some common ways that libraries can apply RWD complete, we can now turn toward some of the specifics as we hear from practitioners about how they think about RWD and why libraries should apply the RWD model. These case studies cover a variety of libraries, but the approaches and advice are adaptable to all types of organizations. Within this discussion, we'll get a better sense of how RWD can be implemented successfully and hear firsthand accounts about what works and things to look out for as you start developing with RWD. As I had conversations with practicing library Web developers, I started to see some themes emerge around library sites being loose affiliations of stitched-together content, how much site loading and performance matters, the need to start small and simply with RWD, and the changing expectations of the mobile user.

The first project is the RWD Web site redesign project from Erin White, Web systems librarian and assistant professor at Virginia Commonwealth University Library. The site is available at www.library.vcu.edu/. Erin answered a few questions about her design thinking as they approached a redesign of the primary Virginia Commonwealth University Library Web site. When asked specifically about "gotchas" that libraries might keep in mind when getting started with RWD, Erin suggests, "don't make your primary Web site your first responsive design project. Do a smaller site or subset of pages first, find out what works for you, then do the big project." She also mentions looking at performance and building the ubiquitous library carousel with it in mind: "performance is just as important as responsive design for all devices. We have a large image carousel on our site and we really worked to get the code and the image file sizes down for faster loading on all devices." When I asked about a single piece of advice that she wanted to share after completing the project, Erin brought up a great point about context: "Don't assume that device equals context. When you can, provide ways for everyone to do everything they need to do, regardless of device. Five years ago we could reasonably assume that a lot of users were using their mobile devices because they were on the go and needed a quick snippet of information: in libraries' cases, looking up a call number, finding library hours, reserving a study room, and so on. Now we use mobile from everywhere and in any context." As we turned toward the end of our conversation, I asked Erin her thoughts about the future of RWD in libraries. She focused on some coming changes and some of the political decisions we make when we design for certain devices: "I think we are peeking at the edges of the transformation phase of responsive Web design. My guess is that it'll mean we think beyond Web pages as pages and try to streamline our sites and applications based on workflows and tasks. . . . We'll need to figure out what to leave behind as we move forward with responsive. And we'll need to remember that there are a bunch of equity issues inherent in choosing what devices or browsers to support."

The second project is the RWD information kiosk project from Amanda L. Goodman, user experience librarian at Darien Public Library. I love this project because it showcases a public library doing some amazing work, and it really demonstrates how RWD can be adapted to nontraditional screens. Amanda built a touchscreen interface for the kiosk that allows you to see maps, ask a librarian, and get a sense of current events. You can see some screenshots of the project on Amanda's blog at www.godaisies.com/2014/07/14/almost-done-the-touchscreen-kiosk/. When considering particular library questions related to RWD, Amanda had an interesting take on what it means to advocate for RWD: "From a buy-in perspective, you may have to deal with people who believe you should have a mobile app to handle mobile users. RWD is more expensive than a traditional one-size-doesn't-fit-all approach and takes more time to implement, but . . . a single responsive Web site is likely to fulfill the needs of a larger audience without the need of maintaining multiple apps for different operating systems." Her single piece of advice after finishing the project was to "load your code responsibly. I have read conflicting strategies, but my favorite is to make the mobile CSS the default style—that is minimum. What you are trying to avoid is your RWD site sending the same number of bytes to a mobile device as it would to a desktop. Anyone trying to watch videos at a bus stop knows that the mobile network is not as fast as your home or work WiFi connection." As for the future of RWD, Amanda notes the current trends around RWD as an expectation: "I listen to Web-centric podcasts and a recurring theme is designers no longer asking clients if they would like their Web site to be responsive. Responsive is now the default. Yet only 12 percent of Web sites are responsive as of January 2014" (www.guypo.com/rwd-ratio-in-top-100000-websites-refined/).

The third project is a library Web subsite design project from Michael Schofield, Web services librarian at Alvin Sherman Library at Nova Southeastern University. Michael has been working hard to streamline the library home page (http://public.library.nova.edu) and to take a critical RWD perspective to the library program and events pages (http://public.library.nova.edu/events). The result is a striking, clean design for two library pages that can often be a muddle of links and information. When thinking about particular library gotchas in implementing RWD, Michael offered a reminder to think about how you present your RWD project: "The politics of the design committee or otherwise among library stakeholders can really derail a project. It may be the designer's wish to build a fast, mobile-first Web site, but if she or he fails to convince the stakeholders, then all they see is a Web site with minimal bling. Libraries redesign to feel current and up with the times, so many of the design decisions that come from responsive Web design will feel counterintuitive. The trick is the pitch." After finishing the project, he offers a solid piece of advice about setting project expectations: "Set some axioms before you break ground on the project. These are rules that are core to your strategy to which future decisions have to adhere. They can be simple statements or performance budgets. I usually go with these three: (1) This will be mobile first. (2) This will be user-experience driven. (3) This will load in three seconds from a phone. These force tough decisions, especially for stakeholders who might not be with the program." In looking toward the future of RWD, Michael offers some perspective on the Web of data as a trajectory for RWD: "As the landscape of screen devices gets increasingly weirder, responsive Web designers have to come to grips with the fact that the Web isn't a small, medium, or large screen—it's content decoupled from presentation. Semantic Web and linked data is what your smart watch or eyewear will use to retrieve content. Even now, if your library hours are properly marked up, the user's query may never get further than Google's search results, which extract and present the information the user cares about before ever getting to the Web site. So the future of responsive Web design is COPE: create once, publish everywhere."

The fourth project is a library Web design project from Sean Hannan, senior web developer at Johns Hopkins University (JHU) Library. Sean talks about RWD as it applies to the academic research portal he built using APIs and Web services from third-party products to "mash up" research databases, LibGuides, and a discovery layer to create a cohesive and fast user experience at www.library.jhu.edu/. This is an interesting project because Sean made a decision to gain some control over the look and feel of the JHU library Web site as well as the performance of the site by reworking some of its data sources. When I asked about the peculiar circumstances of bringing RWD into library applications, Sean noted that "libraries are heavily reliant on vendor software for varied aspects of their day-to-day business. Working with these different platforms gives different experiences when it comes to RWD. The library Web site, for example, could be completely responsive, but as soon as you click over to the catalog, it's not. It's a tough act to balance. In some instances here, we opted to pull content in over vendor APIs so that we would have more control over the presentation. That's an option. More broadly, it will likely involve a negotiation of 'Is this an acceptable experience?' among technical staff, stakeholders, and vendors." When I asked him what general advice he had gleaned from the project, Sean answered: "Test on as many devices as you can. Something well-tested on iOS resolutions is bound to look funky on some Android devices. Also, do thorough desktop testing. I've seen Windows snap-to-edge window sizing trigger some breakpoints that it really shouldn't have." In looking toward the future of RWD, Sean focused on where RWD might go with media objects: "I see a lot of work in the RWD community around responsive images (the <picture> element, etc.). This is going to be integral for the next few phases of RWD, but it will have a hard time getting there without automated tools to generate the appropriate assets and the knowledge of when to use it appropriately."

The final project is an RWD Web site design project from Matthew Reidsma, Web services librarian at Grand Valley State University (GVSU) Library. Matthew was one of the first librarians to grasp the concepts of RWD and promote the practice widely in library site design. With the GVSU library Web site (www.gvsu.edu/library/), Matthew put his theories into practice and built a cohesive, multiple platform experience for library content. In thinking about the uniqueness of RWD library projects, Matthew noted that one of the first challenges he faced was the fact that "library 'Web sites' are really a bunch of different components stuck together to attempt a somewhat cohesive experience, so often a responsive project ends up being a redesign of three or four systems, with different styles written for each to give them the same appearance. It's crazy, really, but also fun. I usually recommend folks start gradually: make your CMS responsive first but wait on the catalog or the ILL software. Start with one system, get comfortable, and then move on to the others." When I asked what general advice he had to offer about RWD, Matthew offered some guidance on breakpoints: "Don't get fixated on the three classes of devices that are common today: desktops, tablets, and smartphones. Designing layouts to 'fit' these three devices isn't really any different than designing one layout to fit a desktop. You don't know what new devices will come out next year, so your layout should match your content, not some arbitrary device." In looking toward the future of RWD, Matthew focused on the interesting problem of performance: "I think performance will become a bigger factor in coming years. I've also been closely watching the development of responsive images. I think performance and responsive images are closely related, so I'm anxious to see the browser makers agree on and implement a standard. In that same direction, I'd love to see a way to test connection speeds from the browser, for determining what assets to load. But that's kind of a dream of mine. Some folks have been experimenting with this, but nothing usable has come out yet."

Distilling the Advice from Our Practitioners on RWD Resources and Tools

In closing out this chapter, I didn't want to miss out on an opportunity to hear from our library developers about their favorite tools, frameworks, or development processes for RWD. This is an extension of our work in chapter 3 on RWD resources, but we get an insider perspective from our own library developers. So without further ado, here's what I found. Erin White talked about process and automation: "We're not using a responsive framework but we are using SASS as a way to manage the massive bundle of CSS issues that come with designing across screen sizes and browsers. We are also using version control, which has saved our bacon multiple times. Bottom line, use tools and automate when you can. The time spent learning a new technology will pay off in spades." Amanda Goodman listed one of her favorite resources and her top framework: "Responsive by Brad Frost (http://bradfrost.github.io/this-is-responsive/): I subscribe to his newsletter. Bootstrap (http://getbootstrap.com/): It's overused, but Bootstrap is a great prototyping tool. You can quickly build out a site in the browser (my favorite way to 'think out loud' about a design) and then tweak the code to fit your needs." Michael Schofield pointed to his favorite CSS processing tool and where he goes to keep up on design and development: "Sass (http://sass-lang.com/) and CSS-Tricks (https://css-tricks.com/). To me, Sass is crucial for writing lean and maintainable CSS. I also use Autoprefixer (https://github.com/postcss/autoprefixer), so I never prefix things—that helps. CSS-Tricks is sort of a cop-out resource, I guess, but for most design elements you don't need JavaScript. And when the most important feature of responsive Web design is its speed, the fewer resources you load, the better. Off-canvas navigation doesn't require scripts; carousels don't even require scripts. More importantly, Chris Coyier of CSS-Tricks curates excellent content and he's dedicated to maintaining even the old stuff. It's a super resource that resists being dated." Sean Hannan brought up a familiar framework and an RWD HTML starter kit: "Initializr (www.initializr.com/): a custom build of HTML5 Boilerplate for your needs. Great way to kickstart a project. And Bootstrap (http://getbootstrap.com/), I guess. Bootstrap gets a lot of flak due to its popularity, but that popularity also means really stellar documentation and a big community to draw from when you really need it." Finally,

Matthew Reidsma points to a browser extension for checking RWD breakpoints, the benefits of keeping things simple, and a performance testing tool: "I'm not a fan of frameworks and plugins, since they offer a one-size-fits-all approach and I feel that your content should guide your layout, but I do make a lot of use of a few Chrome plugins for testing. The first is Dimensions (https://chrome.google.com/webstore/detail/dimensions/baocaagndhipibgklemoalmkljaimfdj), a plugin for measuring things on the screen. This is really useful when I am working on breakpoints. The other is Google Page Speed (https://developers.google.com/speed/pagespeed/). I'm a strong proponent of responsive design as more than just layout—in fact I think performance is almost more important. Page Speed helps me run quick tests on how well optimized my designs are."

5

STEP-BY-STEP LIBRARY PROJECTS
Responsive Web Design (RWD) in Practice

5.1 ADAPTING YOUR EXISTING LAYOUT INTO A RESPONSIVE LAYOUT—A RWD RETROFIT

View the demo:
www.lib.montana.edu/~jason/files/rwd-retrofit/
Download the files:
https://github.com/jasonclark/rwd-retrofit
   or
www.lib.montana.edu/~jason/files/rwd-retrofit.zip

We often work within vendor settings in our library application development. That is, we are often working to integrate "built systems" that have been purchased to provide one of our library services. Some examples of these "built systems" might include our integrated library systems (http://en.wikipedia.org/wiki/Integrated_library_system) or course guide implementations such as LibGuides from SpringShare (http://springshare.com/libguides/). And it's not just libraries; many businesses purchase systems to help workflows and enhance services. Anyone who has purchased a content management system (CMS) has had to integrate the default CMS look and feel into the brand and themes of existing Web sites and services. With this project, we look at some of the challenges and solutions for adapting legacy and external systems into designs that work responsively. The goal is first to distill principles of RWD that can be applied to built systems and then to determine what to look for to make these default designs responsive. Our case study is remaking a fixed-width digital library application into a responsive digital library application for multiple screens (http://arc.lib.montana.edu/national-park-service-webcams/item/7).

When referring to "page" in this chapter, I am talking about this item page with three columns, a fixed header, and a fixed footer. In this chapter, the takeaway is a road-map document showing the principles of RWD, the problems they correct, and the common solutions to make them responsive. The idea is that you can use the road map when you have to integrate legacy or built systems responsively into your Web site.

Step 1: Set the Viewport to Be Adaptable and Responsive

Our first goal with any retrofit is to make sure our site has some instructions for controlling the width and scale of the browser's viewport—in this case, setting an HTML tag that tells the browser how to control the

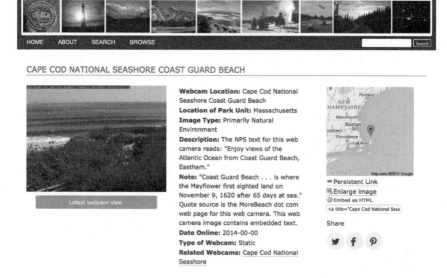

Figure 5.1. Digital Library Application on Large Screen, Item Page without RWD

page's dimensions and scaling. It's a simple tag with incredible power. Hopefully, you have access to the HTML source of the pages to add this tag. This is the simplest means, but you might have to get creative and figure out other ways to edit this tag. Some browsers are starting to implement a viewport declaration (https://developer.mozilla.org/en-US/docs/Web/CSS/@viewport) that might be able to do this in the future: @viewport {width:device-width;}. There are also some possibilities around inserting the <meta> tag with JavaScript (www.quirksmode.org/blog/archives/2011/06/dynamically_cha.html). At any rate, the tag you want to add is below.

```
<meta name="viewport" content="width=device-width, initial-scale=1">
```

Place the **meta viewport** tag inside of the <head> tags at the top of the HTML document to ensure these instructions are found as the page is rendered by the browser. Each of the values inside of the content attribute introduces a specific rule. For example, **width=device-width** tells the page to find and match the screen's width. Once this match is made, it allows the page to adapt content to match different screen sizes. The **initial-scale=1** tag defines the initial scale of the page and the zoom level. Without setting this initial scale, the Web page zooms out in small-screen settings and appears as a tiny version of what you might see on a desktop computer. Add the **<meta name="viewport"** tag to all pages that you are turning into responsive pages. In our digital library application case study, the **meta viewport** tag is added to the head of the document and the first step of our retrofit is in place.

Step 2: Identify Your Method for Assigning Responsive CSS Rules

Our next goal is to figure out how to get our CSS rules onto the page. Two methods are options here. First, we can try to link to new style-sheets that have media queries within the <link> tag to identify when to load and use the styles.

```
<link rel="stylesheet" href="original.css">
<link rel="stylesheet" href="rwd-large.css" media="(min-width:50.1em)">
<link rel="stylesheet" href="rwd-medium.css" media="(max-width:50.1em)">
```

```
<link rel="stylesheet" href="rwd-small.css" media="(max-width:30.063
em)">
```

Note that these new stylesheet calls are placed in the <head> and follow a cascading order to ensure that they override the styles that immediately precede them when a media query is matched to a screen or device. This method works and may be your only option for a retrofit, but it does add three new HTTP requests to your page, which could impact performance. The second method—my preference—involves adding the media queries directly to the original.css document.

```
/* original stylesheet styles */
@media (min-width:50.1em) {
/* large styles*/
}
@media (max-width:50.1em) {
/* medium styles */
}
@media (max-width:30.063em) {
/* smal styles */
}
```

I prefer this method (when I have access to the original stylesheet) because it minimizes the performance hit and keeps the styles isolated in one place. The choice is yours and depends on what files you can access.

Step 3: Set the Base Font Size to the Browser Default

With the meta viewport tag in place and having figured out how to bring in the new CSS rules, we need to set the base font size for the Web browser. Many systems set specific pixel dimensions for their base font size, and when these dimensions are fixed, our responsive design breakpoints have a hard time determining when to flow into the next screen setting. Look in the body and html rules of the original stylesheet to see if you can spot the font-size settings. Once you find it, reset the styles to a relative unit that forces the browser into its default font pixel size of 16 pixels. In this case, you want to set the font size to 100 percent. At 100 percent, the browser uses a size equivalency where 16 pixel ≅ 1 em setting. This sizing equivalency allows us to build our breakpoints around em units, another relative measurement unit. This ties our breakpoints to our content size and makes for a design aligned with type size (an emerging RWD best practice: http://blog.cloudfour.com/the-ems-have-it-proportional-media-queries-ftw/). In our digital library application case study, we switch the font-size:small; to font-size:100%;.

Step 4: Determine and Set the Breakpoints

Our goal has always been to find a way to "linearize" the content on our pages. The single-column pattern works well in medium- and small-screen settings, which are the goal of a retrofit. We haven't seen what happens as we move to a single-column layout, but figure 5.2 gives us a picture of our retrofit redesign on a medium screen.

Before this can happen, we have to determine the dimensions for our breakpoints. Remember I mentioned setting the browser default to 16 pixels. We can use that knowledge to build our breakpoints using the relative em units that work and scale with our typographic settings. Pixels can't do that. So to make our breakpoints, we have to do some division. If we wanted an 800-pixel breakpoint, we would divide 800 by 16 to equal 50. Similarly, for a 480-pixel breakpoint, we would divide 480 by 16 to get 30. You'll see these results expressed in our two media query breakpoints below.

```
/*medium screen view < 801px (based on 16px browser default)*/
@media all and (max-width:50.1em) {
/*medium screen styles here*/
}
/*small screen view < 481px (based on 16px browser default)*/
@media all and (max-width:30.063em) {
/*small screen styles here*/
}
```

We introduce only two breakpoints—medium and small—because our legacy system already has a large-screen view as its default. With these media queries in place, our work to target the problematic page elements with new CSS rules can begin.

Webcam Location: Cape Cod National Seashore Coast Guard Beach
Location of Park Unit: Massachusetts
Image Type: Primarily Natural Environment
Description: The NPS text for this web camera reads: "Enjoy views of the Atlantic Ocean from Coast Guard Beach, Eastham."
Note: "Coast Guard Beach . . . is where the Mayflower first sighted land on November 9, 1620 after 65 days at sea." Quote source is the MoreBeach dot com web page for this web camera. This web camera image contains

Figure 5.2.   Digital Library Application on Medium Screen, Item Page with RWD

Step 5: Identify the Fixed Layout Elements and Rework into Flexible Blocks

With the baseline RWD work done, we are ready to move on and find the specific HTML elements on the page that don't allow the page content to reflow into linear, stacked elements. Typically, these might be grid-like content elements including but not limited to content columns, search result pages, lists of items, data tables, and so on. Try to identify these items in your own site. In our case study, there is a primary grid of three items on our items page. We are going to rework those grids into a single column suitable for medium and small screens.

Our first step is to find the HTML markup and the CSS rules that form the grid layout. You can do this by using your browser's developer tools. Use the "View > Developer Tools" menu in Chrome and the "Tools > Web Developer" menu in Firefox. Figure 5.3 shows how to use Google Chrome's developer tools to inspect the page elements. When you think you have a match, use the magnifying glass icon to select the HTML element and all the associated CSS rules are listed.

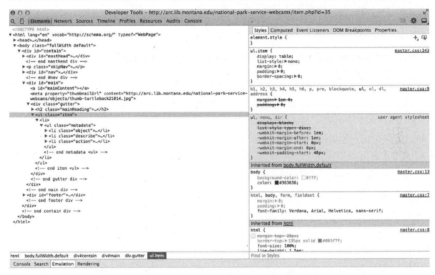

Figure 5.3.   Google Chrome Developer Tool View—HTML and CSS Selection

From this inspection, we can see that the three-column grid for the page is created using a mix of CSS table and float layout. It could be worse. Tables flow between screens, but we can do better. Our goal is to turn off the table and float layout, letting the content blocks stretch across the screen. Our CSS media queries get some new rules here to help us accomplish that task.

```
/*medium screen view < 801px (based on 16px browser default)*/
@media all and (max-width:50.1em) {
ul.item li {display:block;}
ul.metadata li.object, ul.metadata li.describe, ul.metadata li.action
{float:none;width:85%;}
}
/*small screen view < 481px (based on 16px browser default)*/
@media all and (max-width:30.063em) {
ul.item li {display:block;}
```

```
ul.metadata   li.object,   ul.metadata   li.describe,   ul.metadata   li.action
{float:none;width:85%;}
}
```

For both breakpoints, we turn off the table and float styles using the
display:block; and float:none; rules. These rules create our single-column
layout in figure 5.2. These types of rules are what you would use to
create a single-column retrofit of another site as well.

Step 6: Find the Common Fixed-Width Elements and Reset As Flexible Width

Another step in the retrofit process is the incorporation of flexible media objects. This is the second component of the RWD model (fluid
grid layouts, flexible media objects, and media queries). It is part of the
model because common elements such as images and video are often
set up as having a defined width. So a generic goal here is to come up
with a set of CSS rules that can redefine those widths as relative. We'll
work through an image example, but these rules can be applied to other
items that you might want to set up as responsive. Again, using our
browser developer tools, we can see that our images are set to a fixed
width. We'll want to change that by adding a new class to our media
queries.

```
.img-responsive {
display:block;
height:auto;
width:100%;
max-width: 100%;
}
```

We will pair that new class with a new HTML class on any <img> tag
that we want to be flexible.

```
<img class="img-responsive" src="..." />
```

With the CSS and HTML in place, images start to flex in any screen
according to their settings.

This CSS/HTML pattern will work for other media objects as well; you might try setting up a very generic .responsive class with similar CSS rules that you can attach to any item you want to adapt to screen size.

Step 7: Make a Flexible Header and Footer, Including Global Navigation

In our example, there are a few more fixed items to modify. First, it has a giant header image that will not work on medium or small screens. It also has long titles and body text that will break the design on smaller screens. Finally, it has a global navigation and a footer that are fixed to a

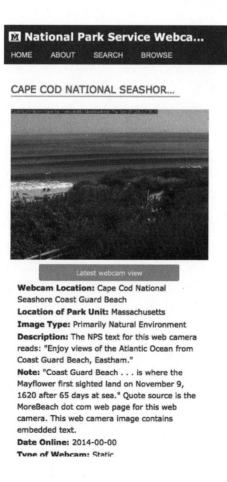

Figure 5.4. Digital Library Application on Small Screen, Item Page with RWD

widescreen view. In order to make the small-screen view that we saw in figure 5.4, there are a couple more additions to make to the CSS rules. About that header: let's remove the image, add ellipses when the header text hits a breakpoint, and slide the global navigation together to fit on smaller screens.

```
div#mastHead {height:45px;}
#mastHead img {display:none;}
#mastHead h1 a {color:#fff;line-height:normal;text-decoration:none;padding-
left:33px;}
h1.visuallyhidden
{border:0 auto;width:100%;height:auto;margin:0;padding:0;opacity:1;clip:
auto;color:#fff;width:750px;white-space:nowrap;overflow:hidden;text-over-
flow:ellipsis;}
```

Note that we set **display:none;** to hide the image. We also need to add a **.visuallyhidden** class to our <h1> tag to make it place ellipses when text flows off the screen. We use this same set of styles in the **.visuallyhidden** class to make our body titles adaptable. The global navigation and the footer are using a float layout, and we can adapt that layout to fit on smaller screens.

```
#nav ul li#searchForm {float:left;width:auto;}
#footer ul li#links {float:left;width:auto;}
```

We can push the links and search form in the header closer together by switching the float to appear next to the other items. We follow a similar pattern as we reset the CSS rules in the footer. With those final rule changes in place, the final medium-screen CSS looks something like the sample below. (Note: the small-screen CSS rules are almost identical.)

```
/*medium screen view < 801px*/
@media all and (max-width:50.1em) {
ul.item li {display:block;}
ul.metadata li.object, ul.metadata li.describe, ul.metadata li.action
{float:none;width:85%;}
.img-responsive {display:block;height:auto;width:100%;max-width:100%;}
div#mastHead {height:45px;}
#mastHead img {display:none;}
```

```
#mastHead h1 a {color:#fff;line-height:normal;text-decoration:none;padding-
left:33px;}
h1.visuallyhidden
{border:0 auto;width:100%;height:auto;margin:0;padding:0;opacity:1;clip:
auto;color:#fff;width:750px;white-space:nowrap;overflow:hidden;text-over-
flow:ellipsis;}
#nav ul li#searchForm {float:left;width:auto;}
#footer ul li#links {float:left;width:auto;}
}
```

Step 8: Thinking about the Generic Techniques of the Retrofit

In the last step of the retrofit, there are a few more takeaways if you
want to think about how to apply these techniques generically. First,
find ways to make things disappear. We did this with display:none; and/
or the opacity:1;clip:auto; for our .visuallyhidden class. Second, allow content to stretch into its container. We did this with our max-width and
width:100%; settings. And finally, reuse existing layouts by changing the
default layout rule. We did this by resetting the table layout to dis-
play:block and by reworking the float layout. Retrofitting is not perfect
and has its limitations, but it can also provide an improved user experience. It is worth learning some of these generic RWD retrofit techniques to give yourself some options to work more flexibly with legacy
systems.

5.2 BUILDING A RESPONSIVE LAYOUT FROM SCRATCH— A RWD BOOKREADER

View the demo:
www.lib.montana.edu/~jason/files/rwd-bookreader/
Download the files:
https://github.com/jasonclark/rwd-bookreader/
   or
www.lib.montana.edu/~jason/files/rwd-bookreader.zip

The act of reading is a central activity supported by libraries. In fact, as
a library service, readers' advisory—the practice of conducting a reference interview to find out people's interests and tastes and offering

books to read—has been a component of public library reference services going back to the beginning of the twentieth century (Wayne Wiegand and Donald Davis, eds., *Encyclopedia of Library History* [New York: Taylor & Francis, 1994], 538). Beyond the recommendation model implied in the readers' advisory interaction, a primary component of library service is supporting long-form reading. E-books and the rise of digital literature pose an interesting problem to enabling reading on multiple screens and platforms. In this project, we build an RWD prototype site from scratch. The goal of the project is to design a book-reader interface that works seamlessly for users across screens and platforms.

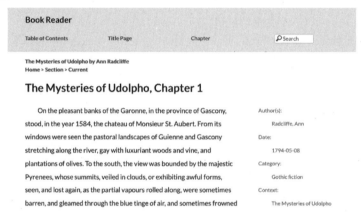

Figure 5.5.   Web Bookreader Interface on Large Screen

The Mysteries of Udolpho, Chapter 1

On the pleasant banks of the Garonne, in the province of Gascony, stood, in the year 1584, the chateau of Monsieur St. Aubert. From its windows were seen the pastoral landscapes of Guienne and Gascony stretching along the river, gay with luxuriant woods and vine, and plantations of olives. To the south, the view was bounded by the majestic Pyrenees, whose summits, veiled in clouds, or exhibiting awful forms, seen, and lost again, as the partial vapours rolled along, were sometimes barren, and gleamed through the blue tinge of air, and sometimes frowned with forests of gloomy pine, that swept downward to their base. These tremendous precipices were contrasted by the soft green of the pastures and woods that hung

Figure 5.6.   Web Bookreader Interface on Medium Screen

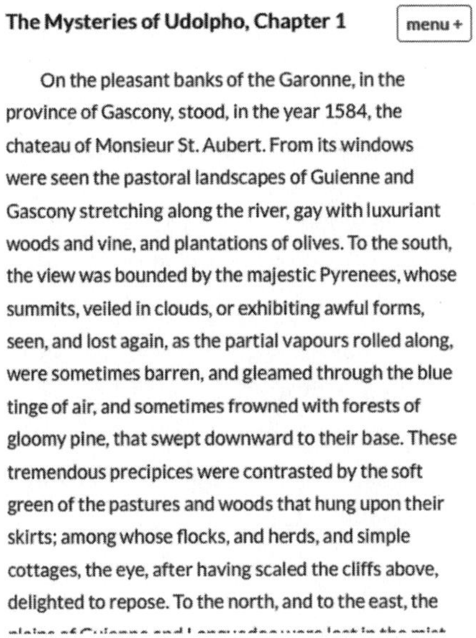

The Mysteries of Udolpho, Chapter 1   menu +

On the pleasant banks of the Garonne, in the province of Gascony, stood, in the year 1584, the chateau of Monsieur St. Aubert. From its windows were seen the pastoral landscapes of Guienne and Gascony stretching along the river, gay with luxuriant woods and vine, and plantations of olives. To the south, the view was bounded by the majestic Pyrenees, whose summits, veiled in clouds, or exhibiting awful forms, seen, and lost again, as the partial vapours rolled along, were sometimes barren, and gleamed through the blue tinge of air, and sometimes frowned with forests of gloomy pine, that swept downward to their base. These tremendous precipices were contrasted by the soft green of the pastures and woods that hung upon their skirts; among whose flocks, and herds, and simple cottages, the eye, after having scaled the cliffs above, delighted to repose. To the north, and to the east, the

Figure 5.7.   Web Bookreader Interface on Small Screen

This challenge is perfect for teaching us how to apply RWD from scratch. Ultimately, we have a Web site that shows us how to apply the first principles of the RWD model. More broadly, we have worked to create an application that answers a question many businesses are trying to answer today: how do we support comfortable and accessible screen reading?

Step 1: Setting Up the Foundational HTML

As mentioned in the introduction, we are working from a downloaded code template to develop our prototype bookreader interface. The customized files are available at www.lib.montana.edu/~jason/files/rwd-bookreader.zip. Unzip the files and open the following files in your text editor.

- index.html
- /meta/styles/master.css
- /meta/scripts/main.js

Our first step works with the HTML. We're going to unpack why the basic HTML markup is set up the way it is in the index.html file. First things first, we need to add a <meta> tag that triggers a responsive design.

```
<meta name="viewport" content="width=device-width, initial-scale=1">
```

With the <meta name="viewport"> tag in place, we turn toward creating HTML that can represent book content. If you think through the pieces of a traditional print book, some components rise to the top as primary sections of a template: a masthead, the table of contents (navigation), a content body, marginalia and appendix, and a footer. We have re-created those divisions here and I point to each section to provide a sense of the backbone of our HTML book template. Our masthead is represented in the HTML as a <header> tag.

```
<header role="banner">
... MASTHEAD CONTENT HERE ...
</header>
```

Full title, author, and some basic navigation components appear here. Our next bit of HTML markup is equivalent to our table of contents (global navigation) and it is shown below.

```
<section id="menu" role="navigation">
<h2>Book Reader</h2>
<nav epub:type="landmarks">
<ul>
<li><a epub:type="toc" href="#">Table of Contents</a></li>
<li><a href="#">Title Page</a></li>
...
</ul>
</nav>
<a href="#top" class="control close">close</a>
</section>
```

This <section> contains links between pages, search functionality, and a pointer to a hypothetical table of contents here. This menu <section> plays an important role as we move into smaller screens; I'll explain how in a later step. We need a place for our book content to appear and the next <main> and <section> tags provide a space to hold our reading material.

```
<main data-bookmark="#"  id="top"  epub:type="bodymatter  chapter"
role=
"main">
<a href="#menu" class="control open">menu</a>
<h1 epub:type="title">ADD TITLE HERE...</h1>
<section class="reading-view">
<div class="reading pane" property="text">
... READING CONTENT HERE ...
</div>
</section>
</main>
```

Most books have a container to hold metadata and supplementary information. We have added an <aside> element to hold marginalia and appendix information about our book chapter.

```
<aside class="metadata pane" epub:type="help appendix" role=
"complementary">
<dl>
<dt>Author(s): </dt>
<dd property="creator">... METADATA HERE ...</dd> <dt>Date: </dt>
<dd property="datePublished">... METADATA HERE ...</dd>
...
<dt>Page: </dt>
<dd class="pagination" epub:type="pagebreak">... PAGE NUMBER HERE
...</dd>
</dl>
</aside>
```

The final bit of HTML markup is some space to hold our page ending information—things like copyright, license information, a link to acknowledgments, internal links to the top of the page to allow users to skip back to the beginning, and so forth. In our template, we have translated this container into a <footer> element.

```
<footer role="contentinfo">
<ul class="info-links">
<li><a href="#top">Top of Page</a></li>
<li><a epub:type="toc" href="#">Table of Contents</a></li> <li><a
epub:type="other-credits" title="CC BY 3.0 US" property="license"
href=https://creativecommons.org/licenses/by/3.0/us/"> License</a></li>
```

```
<li property="publisher provider">My Library</li>
</ul>
</footer>
```

As we get further into the tutorial and after picking some source book material (coming in steps 2 and 3), you can add the details of your own content into all of these HTML containers.

Step 2: Pick a Source File from Project Gutenberg and Add It to the Template

Our next step is to gather some source content for our reading interface. There are a number of possible sources and one of my favorites is Project Gutenberg (www.gutenberg.org/wiki/Gutenberg:Project _Gutenberg_Needs_Your_Donation), which has more than 46,000 books digitized and available for use in multiple formats ranging from Epub (.epub), Kindle format, and plain text (.txt). Try running a search for your favorite book (www.gutenberg.org/ebooks/). Once you find a source, check to make sure it has a plain text (.txt) format available, as we are going to use it to paste into our foundational HTML from step 1 and build a first chapter. In the downloaded code, I chose the *The Mysteries of Udolpho* by Ann Ward Radcliffe (www.gutenberg.org/ ebooks/3268). Browsing through the plain text version of the book, I grabbed some sample text and copied it to my clipboard. Feel free to do the same with your book content. Once you have selected some text, head back to your text editor and look for the reading-view section of the document. It will look like the markup below.

```
<section class="reading-view">
<div class="reading pane" property="text">
```

Inside of this markup, you can start to build the chapter wrapping each paragraph in <p> tags as in the example below.

```
<p>
On the pleasant banks of the Garonne, in the province of Gascony, stood, in
the year 1584, the chateau of Monsieur St. Aubert. From its windows were
seen the pastoral landscapes of Guienne and Gascony stretching along the
river, gay with luxuriant woods and vine, and plantations of olives. To the
```

```
south, the view was bounded by the majestic Pyrenees, whose summits,
veiled in clouds, or exhibiting awful forms, seen, and lost again, as the
partial vapours rolled along, were sometimes barren, ...
</p>
```

Feel free to add as much as you like, but make sure that it is enough to have some reading weight (three or four paragraphs), because we want to test the prototype's user experience of reading on multiple screens. Note that you can add more chapters and link among them to create a full book model as time permits later. For now, we are focusing on building a prototype chapter.

Step 3: Add Some Metadata about Your Book in the \<aside\> Column

With some content identified, it's time to add some descriptions about that content and create a supplementary section that uses a second column in large-screen views of our book. Look for the \<aside\> element and add the information about your book content there.

```
<aside class="metadata pane" epub:type="help appendix" role=
"complementary">
<dl>
<dt>Author(s): </dt>
<dd property="creator">... METADATA HERE ...</dd> <dt>Date: </dt>
<dd property="datePublished">... METADATA HERE ...</dd>
...
<dt>Page:</dt>
<dd class="pagination" epub:type="pagebreak">... PAGE NUMBER HERE
...</dd>
</dl>
</aside>
```

Step 4: Setting the Breakpoints and Creating Fluid Layouts

With our HTML template set up and content in place, we now turn toward setting our CSS rules to make the content readable and "flowable" between screens. Here's where the rubber meets the road and we apply the RWD model to make things go. Our goal is a two-column fluid layout for large screens and a single-column layout for medium and small screens. In your text editor, switch to the /meta/styles/master.css file to follow along. There are a number of global styles in the CSS, but one of the most important is the default font size.

```
body  {background:#fff;color:#000;font-family:Lato,"Helvetica  Neue",Arial,
Helvetica,sans-serif;font-size:100%;}
```

We add it to the <body> tag style to force the browser to render with a 16-pixel default font size. We use this equivalency to set our breakpoints in ems (where 1 em = 16 pixels). Our default styles are for the large screen, which can accommodate two columns. If you think back to our HTML foundation, we are going to lay out the <header>, <main>, <section id="menu" role="navigation">, <aside>, and <footer> elements. We are going to use the CSS display:table property to help us create columns and headers. The <section id="menu" role="navigation"> gets first billing here as it is our primary navigation and label for the content on all of our screen views. The two-column large-screen layout has the following styles.

```
body {display:table;}
[role="navigation"] {display:table-caption;min-height:0;}
[role="navigation"] h2 {-webkit-column-span:all;-moz-column-span:
all;column-span:all;}
[role="navigation"] nav {margin-left:-2.5em;-webkit-columns:4 10em;-
moz-columns:4 10em;columns:4 10em;}
```

With the display:table-caption rule, the <section> sits at the top of the page. Our other page divisions are styled as block-level elements and the two columns for the reading content and metadata content are put in place with the rules below.

```
.reading-view {display:table;font-size:1.25em;line-height:1.938em;min-
height:100%;width:100%;}
.reading-view p {text-indent:1.875em;}
.pane {display:table-cell;text-align:left;vertical-align:top;}
.reading.pane {padding-right:3em;}
```

With our large-screen layout in place, we turn toward making our design fluid as it moves into smaller screens. The first set of rules here is to overwrite the two-column layout for medium screens based on a 50-em breakpoint (based off our default font setting: 1 em = 16 pixels; 800/16 = 50).

```
/*medium screen view < 801px (based on 16px browser default)*/
@media all and (max-width:50.1em) { [role="banner"],[role="contentinfo"]
{display:none;}
.enhanced [role="main"] {border-right:1px solid #d8d8d8;-webkit-transi-
tion:all .25s;transition:all .25s;width:100%;position:absolute;z-index:
2;top:0;right:0;}
.enhanced [role="navigation"] {border:0 none;min-height:
100%;width:75%;position:absolute;z-index:1;top:0;right:0;}
.enhanced .active [role="main"] {-webkit-transform:translateX(-75%);-ms-
transform:translateX(-75%);transform:translateX(-75%);}
.pane {display:block;width:100%;}
.reading {display:table-caption;}
.reading.pane {border-bottom:1px solid #ccc;margin-bottom:.75em;
padding-right:0;}
.reading-view {font-size:1.5em;line-height:2em;}
.metadata {display:table-footer-group;}
}
```

We actually start to remove some elements here as the smaller screen doesn't have much room for a header and footer. The [role="banner"],[role="contentinfo"] {display:none;} rule takes these sections off the medium and small-screen view. We also turn off the table display using the .pane {display:block;width:100%;} to let the remaining elements fill the screen. Note that this is where the flexibility between screens and the layout becomes fluid. The width:100%; rule assigns a relative unit size that can adapt into whatever screen real estate is available. We follow a similar pattern for the smallest screen, with a small change to the line height and size of the font to allow the design to fit comfortably in a small setting.

Step 5: Creating Flexible Objects and Readable Styles in CSS

As this is a reading interface prototype, we are mindful of typography for ease of reading. In all of our breakpoints, we make adjustments using our media queries to the CSS rules to allow for the best line heights and font sizes given the amount of screen space. Those rules appear below and were calculated using the typography ratio calculator (www.pearsonified.com/typography/).

```
/*large screen typography*/
body {...font-size:100%;line-height:1.5;}
/*medium screen typography*/
.reading-view {font-size:1.5em;line-height:2em;}
/*small screen typography*/
.reading-view {font-size:1.125em;line-height:1.688em;}
```

Finally, in the interest of adhering to the flexible media guidelines of the RWD model, we add a set of rules that allows all images to adjust to screen size.

```
img {border:0;-ms-interpolation-mode:bicubic;height:auto;width:100%;max-
width:100%;}
```

The relative units on the width and max-width enable this adjusting behavior. With that, our review of the primary RWD CSS rules for the prototype is finished. It's my hope that the review helped you become familiar with the RWD model we applied and that you will be able to adapt or add new styles as you see fit once your own content is in place.

Step 6: Creating a Fly-Out Menu for Smaller Screens

There is just one last bit of behavior that we need to mention as the <section id="menu" role="navigation"> is necessary for small-screen navigation, but it has been moved out of the way to make room for the readable content. To make it available, we use a bit of JavaScript that will pull it into view when a button is pushed. In this way, the navigation is always available but out of the way until the reader needs it.

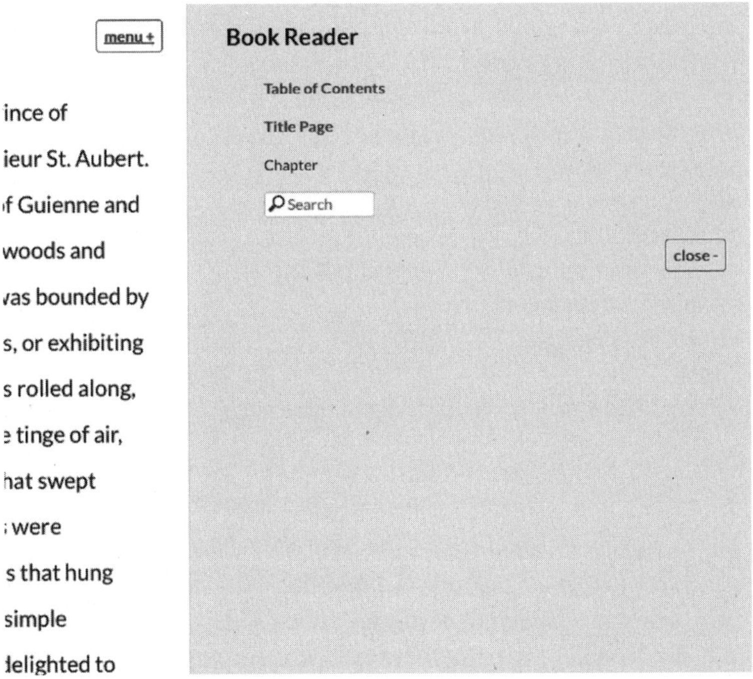

menu +

Book Reader

Table of Contents

ince of

ieur St. Aubert.
Title Page

f Guienne and
Chapter

woods and
Search

vas bounded by

s, or exhibiting

close -

s rolled along,

ɛ tinge of air,

hat swept

ɨ were

s that hung

simple

lelighted to

Figure 5.8. Fly-Out Menus for Web Bookreader Interface on Medium Screen

The button element is an HTML link styled to look like a button that appears in the top right of the screen when we move into the medium and small breakpoints. The HTML markup for the link appears below.

```
<a href="#menu" class="control open">menu</a>
```

Here are the CSS rules that make it appear on those screens.

```
/*medium screen view < 801px (based on 16px browser default)*/
...
.enhanced [role="main"] {border-right:1px solid #d8d8d8;-webkit-transi-
tion:all .25s;transition:all .25s;width:100%;position:absolute;z-index:2
;top:0;right:0;}
.enhanced [role="navigation"] {border:0 none;min-height:100%;
width:75%;position:absolute;z-index:1;top:0;right:0;}
.enhanced .active [role="main"] {-webkit-transform:translateX(-75%);-ms-
transform:translateX(-75%);transform:translateX(-75%);}
```

Note that our [role="navigation"] gets a new class attached to it named .enhanced. If you head over to your text editor and check the JavaScript file (/meta/scripts/main.js_) that we opened in step 1, you will see how this new class is being added.

```
var linkclass = 'control',
activeclass = 'active',
enhanceclass = 'enhanced',
toggleClassName = function(element, toggleClass) {
var reg = new RegExp('(\\s|^)' + toggleClass + '(\\s|$)');
if (!element.className.match(reg)) {
element.className += ' ' + toggleClass;
} else {
element.className = element.className.replace(reg, '');
}
}
```

The JavaScript looks for the <a href="#menu" class="control open"> element and then adds an enhanced class that the CSS rules can pick up and turn on as a displayed item and style. This only happens in the medium and small screens because we set up <a href="#menu" class="control open"> to be hidden on the large screens, since it appears as the global header. This is the power of RWD, which allows you to flip elements from a single HTML file into new shapes, positions, and layouts.

Step 7: Finish Adding Content and Load Files onto a Public Web Server

I'm hopeful that this discussion made you more comfortable with RWD as it might be implemented in a bookreader setting. The major principles are here. It's up to you to experiment and see where you might take these ideas in your own design. The final step is to add more of the content from your source Project Gutenberg file. You might even think about creating additional chapters with a table of contents page to link between them. A fuller prototype using these techniques for a fiction journal is available on the Montana State University Libraries Digital Collections site (http://arc.lib.montana.edu/book/opsis/). When you are finished, move the files onto a public Web server and link them for the world to see and use.

5.3 CREATING A RESPONSIVE CONTACT FORM—"GET A LIBRARY CARD"

View the demo:
www.lib.montana.edu/~jason/files/rwd-form/
Download the files:
https://github.com/jasonclark/rwd-book/
   or
www.lib.montana.edu/~jason/files/rwd-form.zip

The Web as a medium has always been a read and write platform. That is, when we browse and interact with the Web, we act as consumers of the information that we use, but we also are able to create and submit information that makes Web pages do certain things. In the simplest example, a search interaction with Google is one of these moments when we are "writing" new information into the Web. The HTML property that makes this interaction layer possible is the venerable Web <form> (https://developer.mozilla.org/en-US/docs/Web/HTML/Element/form). Given this history, it makes sense for us to turn some attention to designing and building this primary user interaction (UI) layer to work best on multiple devices and screens. In this project, our use case and prototype is a Web form that allows library patrons to sign up for a library card. The form checks for a valid submission and then sends an e-mail to a contact person. The steps detailed below focus on downloading the necessary files for the prototype and explicating the techniques that were applied to create a custom, responsive Web form interface for a library card sign-up routine. Many of the steps are instructive or explanatory and do not require specific edits. When necessary, edits and changes are clearly indicated. The technical requirements for this prototype include HTML, CSS, and PHP (if you want the form to validate the submission and send an e-mail). To get a sense of what we are building, see the two figures below showing what the "Get a Knowledge Card" prototype looks like as it is rendered on multiple screens.

Step 1: Download the Responsive Web Form Template Files

As mentioned in the introduction, we are downloading a "premade" working search app and customizing it for your local Web site. Get the files at www.lib.montana.edu/~jason/files/rwd-form.zip. Unzip the files and open the following files in your text editor.

- index.php
- /meta/styles/master.css

Step 2: Understanding the HTML Foundation of Our Web Form

The foundation of our prototype is HTML, which provides the structure for our display and the various pieces of the user interface. In this case, our interface layer is a Web form built with the following HTML markup in the source file of index.php. Take a look at the index.php file in your text editor. The <main> and <form> tags start at line 19.

```
<div class="main">
<main role="main">
```

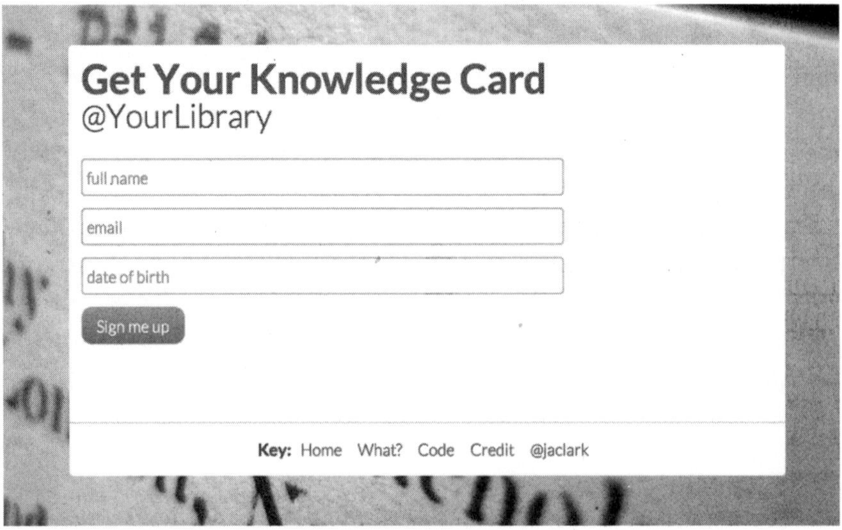

Figure 5.9.   Web Form Interface on Large Screen

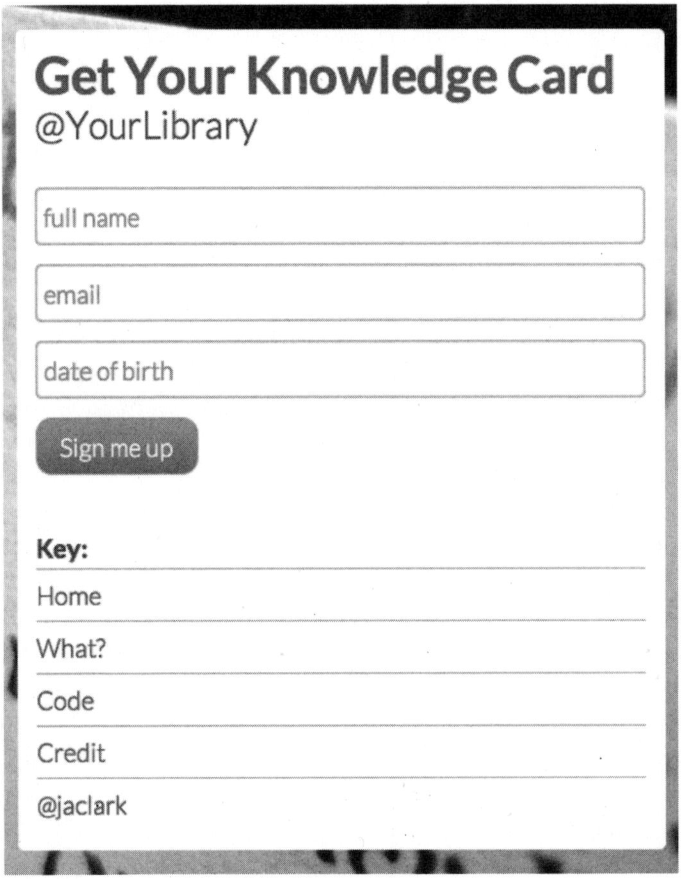

Figure 5.10. Web Form Interface on Small Screen

```
<form method="get" action="index.html">
<fieldset>
<label for="name">Enter full name:</label>
<input type="text" name="name" id="name" placeholder="full name" />
<label for="email">Enter email:</label>
<input type="email" name="email" id="email" placeholder="email" />
<label for="birthday">Enter birthday using YYYY-MM-DD format:</label>
<input type="number" name="birthday" id="birthday" placeholder="date
of birth" />
<button type="submit" class="button">Sign me up</button>
</fieldset>
```

```
</form>
</main>
</div><!--end .main div-->
```

The above code makes our Web form appear in the browser. The <main> element is an HTML5 element that identifies the main content of a page, which is our Web form. The <form> itself is where you can add some of your own language. You might want to add different <label>s or have additional <input>s. We went with a streamlined form that requires only three essential data points: a full name, an e-mail, and a birthday. You could also add your own language to the <button> element if you don't like the call to action "Sign me up." It is important to note that our prototype will not actually process a request until we work through the next step.

Step 3: Understanding the Processing Logic and Setting a Contact Person

The goal with our prototype was to have a <form> to mark up, style, and display responsively, as well as a <form> that actually contacts someone who can register a user. We'll use PHP, a common server-side programming language, to do some very rudimentary processing of the data that comes off the form when it is submitted. Take a closer look at the action on our form from step 2.

```
<form method="get" action="./index.php">
```

When users enter their registration info and touch the "Sign Me Up" button, the action activates a script that makes a request to the internal processing logic on the page. The internal processing logic PHP script checks against a blacklist of bad characters that aren't expected or needed in our registration routine.

```
//declare invalid characters
$badCharacters = "#%*&:;^\/|<>{}";
//validate name, email, and birthdate fields for invalid characters
if (preg_match("/[$badCharacters]/", $_POST['name']) || preg_match("/
[$badCharacters]/", $_POST['email']) || preg_match("/[$badCharacters]/",
$_POST['birthdate'])) {
```

```
echo '<h2>These characters are not allowed or are invalid. </h2>'."\n";
echo '<p>Return to the <a name="back" id="back" href="'.htmlentities
(strip_tags(basename(__FILE__))).'">contact form</a>.</p>';
exit();
}
```

Our final step to make the form work is to set an e-mail for the contact person that might register the user. Another option here would be to allow the registration directly into the catalog or user registration system. I would add a few more checks and validation routines before allowing the form to post directly to the databases, but it is a more efficient option. Anyway, look for the **$mailto** variable to finish this step.

```
$mailto = 'ENTER-YOUR-LIBRARY-CONTACT-EMAIL-HERE';
```

Enter the person's e-mail that you want to receive the registration info. Save the file and once you load it on a public Web server, it will actually process the registration request.

Step 4: Understanding the Header and Footer HTML Markup

A Web page has certain sections that provide context and structure to the page itself. We have looked closely at the <form> markup that creates an interaction layer, but there are additional components to our prototype that create page elements within which the <form> is placed and that work as a composite Web page. The first HTML sections are our <body> and <header> elements.

```
<body class="home" role="document" vocab="http://schema.org/" type-
of="WebPage">
<header role="banner" property="name description">
<h1>Get Your Knowledge Card</h1>
<h2>@YourLibrary</h2>
</header>
```

The <body> element identifies the actual body of the Web page and assigns a type to the page itself using the "**typeof**" attribute with the schema.org vocabulary. The schema.org markup is a semantic vocabulary that helps define the page for robots and search–indexing software agents (e.g., "spiders"). There is additional accessible rich Internet applications (ARIA) markup here in the **"role"** attribute. This attribute tells assistive devices like screenreaders the role that a particular element on the Web page plays. The `<header>` tags and markup contain the titles and subtitles we see displayed when we load the page in the browser. Here again is a point where you might want to change the actual language from "Get Your Knowledge Card @ Your Library" to a more relevant title and subtitle. The final HTML section of note is the `<aside>` markup. Think of this element as the page footer.

```
<aside role="complementary">
<nav role="navigation">
<h3>Key:</h3>
<a href="./index.php">Home</a>
<a href="./what.php">What?</a>
<a href="./code.php">Code</a>
<a title="Bibliography by Suzanne Chapman (CC BY-NC-SA 2.0)"
href="https://www.flickr.com/photos/sukisuki/4413551329/">Credit</a>
<a href=http://twitter.com/jaclark class="twitter">@jaclark</a>
</nav>
</aside>
```

Inside this footer element are components for navigation among the other pages in our Web app. We also see another ARIA role attribute that identifies the `<aside>` as a "complementary" page element. As you develop your own page, you should change the navigation here to enable users to move to the pages within your own Web site.

Step 5: Making the Styles and Responsive Design Using the CSS

With the HTML foundation in place, the next step is to provide the look and feel for the page and then finally to add the rules that make the page display responsively across multiple screens and devices. Take a look at the /meta/styles/master.css file in your text editor. Lines 5 to 37 are the style rules and declarations that create the default screen views for desktop, laptop, and large-screen devices. These styles form the core of our display. Two items are worth noting here. First, the font styles that give the page a clean look are brought in using a call to the Google Fonts API in line 5. There are also some baseline override settings in the CSS, including the assignment of "font-size" with a default size of 100 percent to allow for scaling and a default browser font size to style against.

```
@import
url(https://fonts.googleapis.com/css?family=Lato:300italic,700italic,
300,700);
html,body,div,span,object,iframe,h1,h2,h3,h4,h5,h6,p,blockquote,
pre,abbr,address,cite,code,del,dfn,em,img,ins,kbd,q,samp,small,
strong,sub,sup,var,b,i,dl,dt,dd,ol,ul,li,fieldset,form,label,legend,
table,caption,tbody,tfoot,thead,tr,th,td,article,aside,canvas,
details,figcaption,figure,footer,header,hgroup,menu,nav,section,
summary,time,mark,audio,video{border:0;outline:0;font-size:
100%;vertical-align:
baseline;background:transparent;margin:0;padding:0;}
```

Second, these default styles use percentage widths to create a fluid, flexible container. For example, note how the <body< tag is assigned a percentage "max-width" below.

```
body{font-size:small;font:20px/1.6 Lato, "Helvetica Neue", Helvetica, Arial,
sans-serif;max-width:80%;position:relative;padding:50px;}
```

This fluid and flexible container is what allows our content to flow and shift among screen sizes. Our final step here is to set the breakpoint for the <form> and rest of the page. Our initial style settings in the CSS file allow for our content to flow from large screens into tablets, but we need a more linear set of styles for when our screen starts to get smaller and in the range of smartphones and related devices. Here's where we can apply the media query to introduce a new set of rules for display. At around line 39, you can see the rules that create the breakpoint.

```
/* phone and "phablet" styles */
@media only screen and (max-width: 768px) {
body{padding:20px;max-width:100%;}
main{min-height:250px;}
aside h3,aside a{display:block;}
aside{border:none;}
aside a{border-top:1px solid silver;margin:0;padding:.25rem 0;}
h1{font-size:40px;}
```

```
h2{font-size:30px;line-height:1.2;}
input{width:85%;}
.button{display:block;}
}
```

The media query expression **@media only screen and (max-width: 768px)** establishes that after screen sizes shrink below 768 pixels (an approximation of the screen for tablets), these rules will apply. Note that we move away from allowing elements to span the page and site next to each other using **{display:block;**. Even the **<body>** tag is allowed to stretch completely across the screen viewport based on the **max-width:100%** declaration. This is what I mean by a more linear set of styles where each element gets its own line and the page tends to turn into a scrollable, vertical page rather than a horizontal one. This vertical orientation is perfect for smaller screens and is an established UI pattern for mobile device users. With these final changes, you have a responsive library card sign-up form ready for use across multiple screens and devices.

Step 6: Save the Files and Place on a Public Web Server

My goal with this walkthrough should demonstrate the concepts and markup that could be used to make a library **<form>** responsive. With this foundation in place, you can apply the concepts to your own library **<form>** and integrate the ideas into your local system. Your final step is uploading the HTML and CSS to a public Web directory on your server.

5.4 CREATING A RESPONSIVE SEARCH INTERFACE

View the demo:
www.lib.montana.edu/~jason/files/digital-collections-custom
-search-api/
Download the files:
https://github.com/jasonclark/digital-collections-custom-search-api
   or

www.lib.montana.edu/~jason/files/ digital-collections-custom-search
-api.zip

Search and discovery remain a core service of libraries, and people are searching whenever and wherever they can. More and more, this means that the interaction of search is being performed on all kinds of devices and screens. In this project, we look at how to use the Google Custom Search API and RWD principles to build a search of your library Web site for multiple platforms and screens. (API stands for application programming interface. In simple terms, an API is a set of rules or functions that allows one computer system to access data and services from another remote computer system.) This Web app searches against a Google Custom Search index of your library Web site and creates a display that works for multiple platforms and screens. The steps detailed below focus on downloading the necessary files for the application and editing certain pieces of code to create a custom, responsive search interface for your library. In the interest of teaching about how the app was built and works, many of the steps are instructive or explanatory and do not require specific edits. Whenever necessary, edits and changes are clearly indicated. Requirements for this app include PHP, HTML, and CSS, so make sure your local systems support these technologies. (It is a common technology stack, but ask your server administration about support just to be sure.) Here are two screen shots of what a search results page looks like in the app we're customizing.

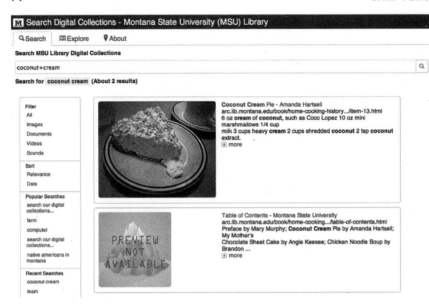

Figure 5.11.   Search Results Screen for Large Screen

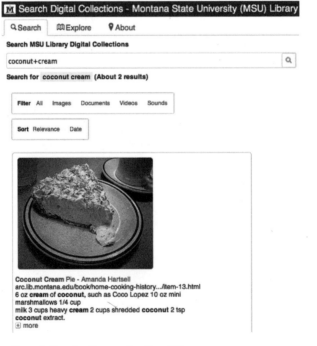

Figure 5.12.   Search Results Screen for Small Screen

Step 1: Getting an Account for the Google Custom Search API and Creating a Search Index

The data source for our app is the Google Custom Search index. We are going to run queries against this index to create search views of data for our application. In order to make these queries for Google Custom Search data, you need to register for an account to create your Google Custom Search index and to use the Google Custom Search API. To sign in using an existing Google account or to create a new one, visit www.google.com/cse/create/new. In the "sites to search" section, add the pages you want to include in your Google Custom Search Engine index. In this case, you will add the base URL for your library's Web site. When finished, name your search engine and press the "create" button. This creates the Google Custom Search Engine index we will use.

Step 2: Get Your Google Custom Search Engine ID and API Key

Your account provides you with a search engine ID and an API key that allows you to access the Google Custom Search API Web service. We use the Web service to query our Google Custom Search Engine and to provide the search results for our responsive search interface. You can get your search engine ID in the Setup > Basics > Details section of the Google Custom Search control panel.

The API key allows Google to monitor your use of their service and to look for your application to show the right credentials for accessing the API. (Full details for getting an API key are available at https://developers.google.com/console/help/new/#generatingdevkeys.) You can get your API key from the Google Developers console at https://console.developers.google.com/. Visit the console, select/create a project. In the sidebar on the left, select "APIs & auth." Next, turn on the "custom search API." In the sidebar on the left, select "credentials," press the "create new key" button, and pick the "browser key" option.

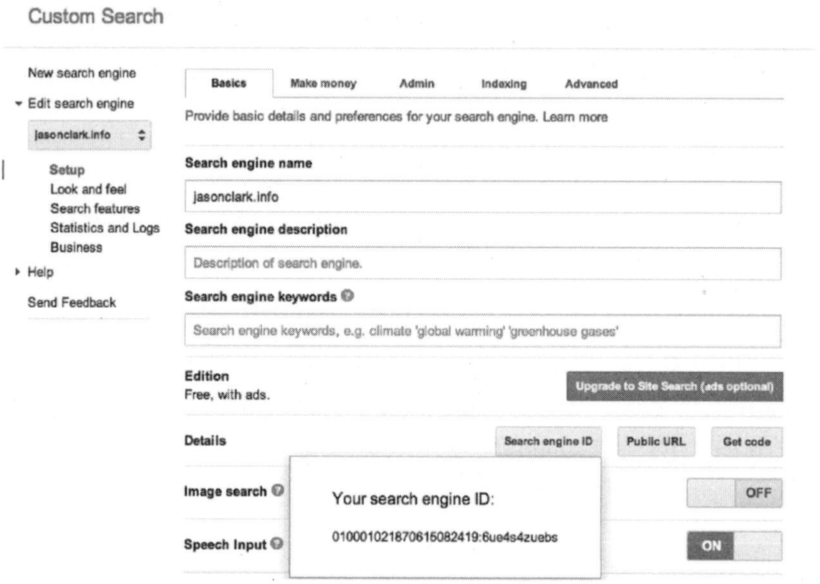

Figure 5.13. Google Custom Search Control Panel

Record your API key in a safe place, as you will need it later. (Full details, documentation, and the terms of service for the Google Custom Search API can be found at https://developers.google.com/custom-search/json-api/v1/overview.)

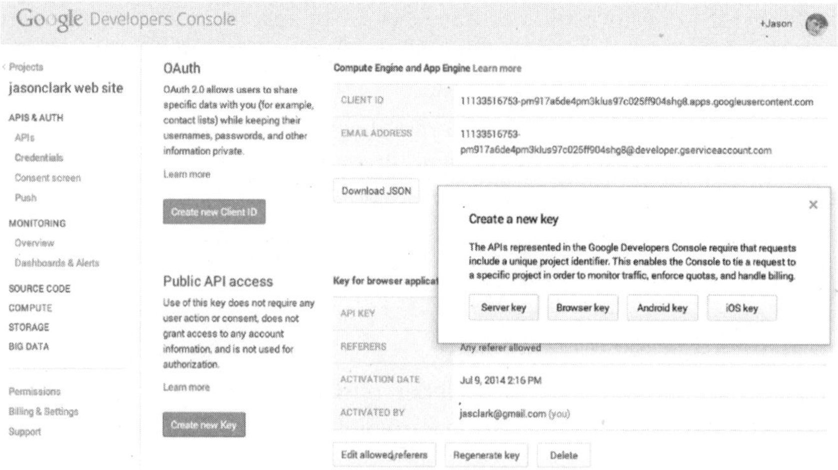

Figure 5.14. Google Cloud Console Panel

Step 3: Download the Responsive Search Template Files

As mentioned in the introduction, we are downloading a "premade" working search app and customizing it for your local Web site. Get the files at www.lib.montana.edu/~jason/files/digital-collections-custom-search-api.zip. Unzip the files and open the following files in your text editor.

- index.php
- /views/search.php
- /views/about.php
- /meta/styles/app.css

Step 4: Building the Responsive Display Interface and Naming the Application

With our Google Custom Search index created and an API key registered, the preliminary work is complete. In this step, we can get started building the app itself. It is useful to think of the app as having two functional components: an interface for displaying search interactions and a processing function where data is requested and parsed. The responsive search interfaces are built with HTML and CSS, while the "back-end" processing functions use PHP to make different views of data appear during different app functions. To illustrate these separate layers of the application, let's take a closer look at the initial page view for the app. At this point, I explain what lines in the files are doing in order to help you learn how the search and display pages are working. No need for edits just yet. Our interface layer is a search form built with the following HTML markup in the source file of /views/search.php:

```
<form id="searchBox" method="get" action="./index.php?view=search">
<fieldset>
<label for="q">Search</label>
<input type="text" maxlength="200" name="q" id="q" tabindex="1" val-
ue="keyword, name, title..." />
<button type="submit" class="button">Search</button>
</fieldset>
</form>
```

The above code makes a search form appear in the browser and it is styled for display using the following CSS styles from the /meta/styles/ app.css file.

```
input,select {vertical-align:middle;border-width:0;}
fieldset {border:0 none;}
form#searchBox {position:relative;width:100%;height:30px;background-col-
or:#fff;border:1px  solid  #ddd;border-radius:3px;-moz-border-radius:3px;-
webkit-border-radius:3px;}
#searchBox label {display:none;}
#searchBox input {position:absolute;top:3px;left:0;margin:0 3px;padding:0;
width:85%;line-height:25px;height:25px;font-size:1.4em;border:0;-webkit-
appearance:none;}
#searchBox button{position:absolute;top:0;right:0;cursor:pointer;margin:0;
padding:0;width:30px;height:30px;float:left;background:
url('../img/search.gif') no-repeat 50% 50%;text-indent:-999em;border:
1px  solid  #ddd;border-radius:3px;-moz-border-radius:3px;-webkit-border-
radius:3px;}
```

And with that, we have our HTML markup and CSS styles for our responsive interface. Note how the width of the #searchBox input is set in percentages. This practice of flexible sizing is a hallmark of RWD and allows the form input to flow and adjust to screen sizes. But we need one more change to customize the application—a unique title or display name. Go to index.php in your text editor and look for lines 2 through 4. The lines should look like this:

```
//set value for title of page
$pageTitle = 'Search Digital Collections - Montana State University (MSU)
Library';
$subTitle = 'app';
```

These lines are the place where you set the display name for your app that will appear at the top of the screen. Add your specific title in the $pageTitle and $subTitle variables, replacing 'Search Digital Collections - Montana State University (MSU) Library' with your unique title. Be mindful of the limited space a mobile device will display. A suggested title might look like:

```
//set value for title of page
```

```
$pageTitle = 'MSU Library Search';
$subTitle = 'Website;
```

One other customization should be made here. We want our links in the footer of our page to point at our full desktop Web site. Look for the following HTML markup near the bottom of the page in index.php.

```
<a accesskey="4" class="class="site icon-browser" " title="full site"
href="/">Full site</a>
<a accesskey="5" class="about icon-info-circle " title="feed for collection"
href="./index.php?view=about "/>About</a>
```

In the first href= value, replace the "/" with the link to your full desktop Web site. After you have settled on your title, your link to your full site, save index.php into the same directory where you unzipped the file in step 3.

Step 5: Building the Search-Processing Layer and Setting Your Google Custom Search Credentials

The processing layer of our application is built around the goal of getting data or results from our Google Custom Search Engine index. Take a closer look at the action on our form from step 2.

```
<form method="get" action="./index.php?view=search">
```

When someone enters a search term and touches the search button, the action—index.php?view=search—activates a script that makes a request to the Google Custom Search API. In this case, our processing layer is a PHP script that is part of the file located at /views/search.php. In steps 1 and 2, we signed up for the Google Custom Search service, created a custom search engine, and got our API key. We are now going to use those credentials to enable our script to make requests to the Google Custom Search API. Lines 31 through 35 in the /views/search.php assign default values and settings for our search-processing functions.

```
// Set user API key for Google Custom Search API
$key = isset($_GET['key']) ? $_GET['key'] : 'YOUR-GOOGLE-CUSTOM-
```

```
SEARCH-API-KEY-HERE';
// Set user ID for Google custom search engine
$id = isset($_GET['id']) ? $_GET['id'] : 'YOUR-GOOGLE-CUSTOM-SEARCH-
ENGINE-ID-HERE';
```

In order to make the script work for your local library, there are two pieces of information that you must add to these credentials. Open up the file named "search.php" in the "views" folder and find the above lines at the top of the script. First, you must add your Google Custom Search API key value to the $key variable. Adding your key validates you as a registered user of the Google Custom Search API and allows you to query the Google Custom Search API Web service for data. Second, you must add your Google Custom Search Engine ID to the $id variable. The $id variable is one of the most essential edits to the existing source code for this application, as it allows the search-processing script to query your Google Custom Search index and make the app work as a local Web site search. When finished with these edits, save "search.php" to the "views" folder.

Step 6: Making Requests to the Google Custom Search API

Our next step in creating a search-processing layer for our app is to use the actual data that someone submitted from the search form to make a request to the Google Custom Search API. The Google Custom Search API is a Web service, which means we can make a request using a specifically formatted URL. We send the formatted URL to the Google Custom Search API and get structured data in return. For most of this step, we are looking at the code that makes things go and exploring what is going on. If a code change is required, it will be indicated.

In our app, we make one of our first calls to the Google Custom Search API to retrieve a list of matching search results based on a query from our search form. Our script uses the values that came from the search form to populate the $q variable. Lines 10 and 11 in our /views/search.php file look like the example below.

```
//set default value for query
$q = isset($_GET['q']) ? trim(strip_tags(urlencode($_GET['q']))) : null;
```

$_GET tells our script to use the values in the URL to assign data to the variables. These variable values were pushed into the URL when our search form was submitted. Another closer look at the search form should help illustrate this.

```
<form id="searchBox" method="get" action="./index.php?view=search">
...
<input type="text" maxlength="200" name="q" id="q" tabindex="1" val-
ue="keyword, name, title..." />
<button type="submit" class="button">Search</button>
...
</form>
```

When the form is submitted, the <input /> values (q) become part of the URL and our script at /views/search.php uses them to create the $q variable. This variable is combined and formatted as a second URL that will be pushed forward to the Google Custom Search API in the following lines (lines 64 and 65) of the /views/search.php file.

```
//set URL for the Google Custom Search API call
$url = "https://www.googleapis.com/customsearch/$v?key=$key&cx=$id&
alt=$form".(is_null($sort) ? "" : "&sort=$sort")."&num=$limit&start=$start
&prettyprint=true&q=$q".(is_null($facet) ? "" : "&hq=$facet");
```

When pieced together, the raw URL request looks like this:

```
https://www.googleapis.com/customsearch/v1?key=  YOUR-GOOGLE-CUS-
TOM-SEARCH-API-KEY-HERE    &cx=YOUR-GOOGLE-CUSTOM-SEARCH-EN-
GINE-ID-HERE&alt=json&num=10&start=1&prettyprint=true&q=jason+clark
```

Let's unpack the parameters in the above URL in order to help us understand how one communicates specific requests to the Google Custom Search API using a URL. The base URL for the Web service is www.googleapis.com/customsearch/v1?, "q" is our query, "alt" is the format of data to return, "key" is our Google Custom Search API key, "cx" is the Google Custom Search Engine index to query, "start" is the first record result number to return, and "num" is the number of record results to return. Once the request is in order, our script passes the URL to the Google Custom Search API. In the interest of instruction, we can look at the response from the API to understand how the whole process works together. Here's an excerpt of the structured data that the request delivers:

```
...
"searchInformation": {
"searchTime": 0.498198,
"formattedSearchTime": "0.50",
"totalResults": "3",
"formattedTotalResults": "3"
},
"items": [
{
"kind": "customsearch#result",
"title": "Jason Clark - Head of Library Informatics and Computing
[Associate ...",
"htmlTitle": "\u003cb\u003eJason Clark\u003c/b\u003e - Head of Library
Informatics and Computing [Associate \u003cb\u003e...\u003c/b\u003e",
"link": "http://www.lib.montana.edu/people/about.php?id=23",
"displayLink": "www.lib.montana.edu",
"snippet": "Jason Clark. Title: Head of Library Informatics and Computing
[Associate \nProfessor]. Department: Library Informatics and Computing,
Montana State \nUniversity.",
"htmlSnippet": "\u003cb\u003eJason Clark\u003c/b\u003e. Title: Head of
Library Informatics and Computing [Associate \u003cbr\u003e\nProfessor].
Department: Library Informatics and Computing, Montana State
\u003cbr\u003e\nUniversity.",
"cacheId": "UwDosyk1vAkJ",
"formattedUrl": "www.lib.montana.edu/people/about.php?id=23",
"htmlFormattedUrl": "www.lib.montana.edu/people/about.php?id=23",
"pagemap": {
"ItemPage": [
{
"thumbnailUrl":   "http://www.lib.montana.edu/people/meta/img/photos/Ja-
sonClark-thumb.jpg"
}
],
"Organization": [
{
"name": "Montana State University (MSU) Library",
"sameAs": "http://www.freebase.com/m/0j3y9r1"
}
```

],
...

The structured data returned from the Google Custom Search API is JSON. You can see that all the information we might want to display about an item is available: title, snippet, URLs, and so forth. Our processing layer now needs to select the pieces of data we want to display in our search results.

Step 7: Parsing the Google Custom Search JSON File to Create a Search Results View

Our next step in building the processing layer is to create our search results view by picking our way and choosing the pieces of data from the Google Custom Search API JSON file that we would like to display. Once again, this step focuses on explaining the code to ensure the reader has a full sense of how the application works. The PHP code that creates our search view by selecting pieces of data from the JSON file shown in step 6 begins around line 70 in the /views/search.php file.

```
//build request and send to Google Ajax Search API
$request = file_get_contents($url);
if ($request === FALSE) {
// API call failed, display message to user
echo '<p><strong>It looks like we can\'t communicate with the API at the
moment. </strong></p>'."\n";
exit();
}
//decode json object(s) out of response from Google Ajax Search API
$result = json_decode($request, true);
//get values in json data for number of search results returned
$totalItems = isset($_GET['totalItems']) ? strip_tags((int)$_GET
['totalItems']) : $result['queries']['request'][0]['totalResults'];
if ($totalItems <= 0) {
// Empty results, display message to user
echo '<p><strong>Sorry, there were no results</strong></p>'."\n";
}
else {
// Make sure some results were returned, show results as html with result
numbering and pagination
```

```
? >
<h2 class="result">Search for <strong><?php echo urldecode($q); ?></
strong> (About <?php echo $totalItems; ?> results)</h2>
...
<ul class="result">
<?php
foreach ($result['items'] as $item) {
$link = rawurldecode($item['link']);
?>
<li>
<p class="result-object">
<a href="<?php echo $link; ?>" >
<img alt="<?php echo htmlentities($item['title']); ?>"
src="<?php $thumbnail =
isset($item['pagemap']['metatags'][0]['thumbnailurl']) ?
$item['pagemap']['metatags'][0]['thumbnailurl'] :
(isset($item['pagemap']['cse_thumbnail'][0]['src']) ?
$item['pagemap']['cse_thumbnail'][0]['src'] :
(isset($item['pagemap']['cse_image'][0]['src']) ?
$item['pagemap']['cse_image'][0]['src'] : './meta/img/thumbnail-
default.png'));echo rawurldecode($thumbnail);?>" />
</a>
</p>
<p class="result-description">
<a href="<?php echo $link; ? > " ><?php echo $item['htmlTitle']; ? ></a>
<br />
<?php echo $item['htmlFormattedUrl']; ? >
<br />
<?php echo $item['htmlSnippet']; ?>
<br />
<?php //echo 'id: '.$sr['cacheId']; ?>
<a class="expand" href="<?php echo $link; ?>" <more</a>
<br />
<br />
</p>
</li>
<?php
}
?>
</ul>
...
```

Some quick notes about what is happening above. The **$request** variable is where we are formatting the URL request and sending it to the Google Custom Search API. When the response from the API is returned, we wrap the request in the **$result** variable and then start to pick our way through the JSON document. We know there are certain pieces of data that we need for our search result display, and our last step here is to start picking the parts of the JSON file that we will need. Our search result display uses the <ul> (unordered list) HTML markup and that's why we use the "echo" statement to print out the beginning of our list.

```
echo '<ul class="result">'."\n";
```

Shortly after, we create a programming loop that works through all the nodes of the JSON document and retrieves the values that we need for our display. The loop starts here:

```
foreach ($result['items'] as $item) {
```

Within the loop we grab the values we need like the title, author, ID, and so on using programming expressions.

```
$item['title']will get the item title
$item['htmlFormattedUrl'] will get the item URL
```

With that, we have created our processing layer that will show our search results display.

Step 8: Applying CSS Media Queries to Create an RWD

Our first goal with this application was to create a usable search experience independent of platform. In other sections of this book, I discussed ways to apply CSS media queries to adapt our display to multiple platforms and screens. In many ways, this is the secret sauce of RWD. We apply it in this responsive search application to make our display move from a stretched, multiple-column layout to a single-column, linear layout. See figures 5.11 and 5.12 to get a sense of these different views of the same data. Within our /meta/styles/app.css file, you can see more clearly how this works. First, we have to set a base level font size for our responsive design in order to have a baseline to react to the changes in screen size. Line 3 in our app.css file creates this baseline.

```
body {font:62.5% normal Helvetica, sans-serif;margin:0;padding:0;overflow-x:hidden;}
```

The specific declaration 62.5% normal tells the Web browser that our later measurement of ems will have size settings of 1 em equaling 10 pixels. This will come in handy when we start to apply our CSS media queries. Our final action in this step is to set the breakpoints for when we want our search layout to move from multiple columns to a single column. Lines 151 to 170 in our app.css file control those breakpoints.

```
@media (max-width:63em)
{
.result-facet {border: none;margin:0 1%;}
.facet-heading {font-weight:bold;margin:0 0 0 1em;}
.facet-filter {margin:.45em;text-indent:0;}
.facet-filter {padding:.5em;}
.facet-link {margin: .25em;padding:.5em;text-indent:0;}
.facet {display: inline-block;}
.result-facet {display:inline-block;width:84%;}
.result-facet p {border: #ccc 1px solid;border-radius:3px;}
.result, #main ul.result li {width:90%;}
ul.pages li {left: 30em;}
.recent, .popular {display:none;}
}
@media (min-width: 1em) and (max-width:50em) {
.result-description {width:80%;}
.result-facet {margin:0 1%;}
.result-facet p {border: #ccc 1px solid;}
ul.pages li {left: 25em;}
}
```

In this case, the @media rule looks for the size of the screen to be smaller than 50 em (500 pixels) or larger than 63 em (630 pixels) to determine when to flow into single or multiple columns.

Step 9: Annotate or Remove the Additional Page Views for the Search Application

Earlier in the tutorial, we mentioned that there were additional page views for the app (e.g., /views/about.php or /views/explore.php). You may want to provide a description for the application if someone wants to learn more about it or who made it. You can do this by adding information to /views/about.php. Open up about.php in the "views" folder and add your library information and a description of the who, what, when, and where of the project. After you have made these edits, save about.php to the views folder. The /views/explore.php file is a browse point that uses info from recent search queries and the most popular search queries on your Google Custom Search Engine to allow people to browse further into the app. It can be left alone or it can be removed entirely if it seems to be causing problems or distractions for your users.

Step 10: Customizing the Look and Feel of the App Using CSS; Loading the App into a Public Web Directory

A final step in customizing the app for your library might be changing colors, link styles, or any other stylistic elements to coordinate your library CSS styles. The files that control these rules in our template app are located at /meta/styles/app.css. Open app.css from the /meta/styles/ directory in your text editor and make any changes you like. Save the file when you are finished. (Note: Tread lightly on the styles that dictate layout, such as: #doc, #hd, #main, and #ft. Significant changes to these CSS rules that govern layout could affect the responsive display.)

Once you are satisfied with the changes, make sure all your open files are saved and then move the whole folder from the template app (with all your customizations and edits) to a public Web directory. You now have a working responsively designed search interface optimized for multiple screens and platforms. (Author note: Thanks to Scott Young [http://scottwhyoung.com/], the digital initiatives librarian at MSU Library, for his consult and early prototyping of the RWD search design when we built a similar search interface for our MSU digital collections at http://arc.lib.montana.edu/digital-collections/.)

5.5 CREATING A RESPONSIVE SINGLE-PAGE APPLICATION—"MOBILE FEED APP"

View the demo:
www.lib.montana.edu/~jason/files/ html5-mobile-feed/
Download the files:
https://github.com/jasonclark/html5-mobile-feed/
   or
www.lib.montana.edu/~jason/files/ html5-mobile-feed.zip

Native apps that run on mobile devices have started to create user experience patterns and expectations about performance for our users. Such software runs quickly and has direct access to all kinds of device software and hardware that make the native app experience hard to beat. One response from the mobile Web development community has been the design of the single-page application (SPA) Web page or Web site that works to seamlessly load page components in the background. The SPA model works by loading only the necessary data into the screen view based on the user's request. Developers that follow the model can craft mobile Web applications that perform and feel closer to a native app experience. Some common single-page application frameworks include jQuery Mobile (http://jquerymobile.com/) and Angular.js (https://angularjs.org/). In this project, we are building a simple single-page application from scratch that allows you to select and load the XML feed and then browse and search through the feed. The app loads the actions and data into the screen only when the user makes a specific request for a particular view of the data. The goal is to introduce this mobile Web application architecture and to provide a way for you to display a blog or Web feed from your library Web site across multiple devices and platforms.

Step 1: Download the Responsive Single-Page Application Template Files

As mentioned in the introduction, we are downloading a working mobile feed app, explaining the code that makes the app work, and customizing it for your local Web site. You can get the files at

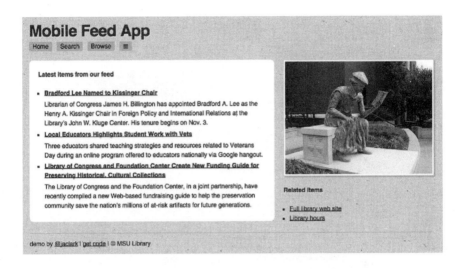

Figure 5.15.   Single-Page App Interface on Large Screen

www.lib.montana.edu/~jason/files/html5-mobile-feed.zip.   Unzip   the
files and open up the following files in your text editor.

- index.html
- /meta/styles/master.css

Step 2: Understanding the HTML Foundation of the Single-Page Application

Our first step in setting up the HTML foundation of the app begins
with the <header> tag, which identifies the main header and name for
the app. Add the name that you want for the app in between the <h1>
tags.

```
<body role="document" vocab="http://schema.org/" typeof="WebPage">
<div id="doc">
<header role="banner" property="name description">
<h1>Mobile Feed App</h1>
</header>
```

The second part of this step involves setting up the main navigation that
allows us to select certain page views. Note that each of the navigation

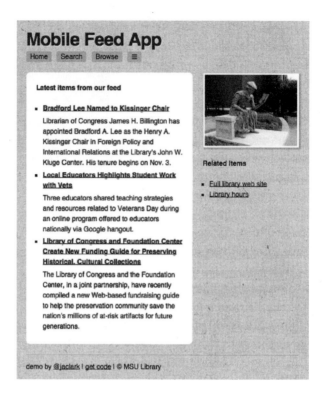

Figure 5.16.   Single-Page App Interface on Tablet Screen

points have # hashes that identify the different page views. A normal
Web application would point to separate HTML pages, but our single-
page application has each HTML section within this HTML file. In this
page architecture we will use the # hashes to pull different sections of
the page into view using JavaScript (which is covered in the step where
we introduce the app behavior).

```
<nav role="navigation">
<ul id="nav" property="breadcrumb">
<li><a href="#home">Home</a></li>
<li><a href="#search">Search</a></li>
<li><a href="#browse">Browse</a></li>
<li<<a href="#set"<&#9776;</a></li>
</ul>
</nav>
```

Figure 5.17. Single-Page App Interface on Small Screen

With the navigation in place, we add a final touch by adding our supplementary image to the page. If you have an image or brand that you would like to appear, feel free to add the image to the src= attribute here.

```
<aside role="complementary">
<figure>
<img property="primaryImageOfPage"
src="./meta/img/reader.jpg" alt="statue of a reader" />
<figcaption>statue of a reader</figcaption>
</figure>
</aside>
```

Step 3: Setting Up the Page Sections for the Single-Page Application

With the initial HTML in place, the next step is crafting the page sections of the application. We begin by setting up the main page container to provide an HTML wrapper around the distinct page views.

```
<div id="main">
<main role="main">
...
</main>
</div><!-- end #main -->
```

With our main page container on the page, we can now work on setting up the page divisions. If you recall from our navigation, there are four sections: home, search, browse, and settings. Each of these page view divisions is shown below using the enclosing <section> tag.

```
<!-- home page -->
<section id="home" role="region" aria-labelledby="home">
<header>
<h2 property="headline">Latest items from our feed</h2>
</header>
<ul id="listView"></ul>
</section>
<!-- search page -->
<section id="search" role="region" aria-labelledby="search">
<header>
<h2 property="alternativeHeadline">Search the latest items... </h2>
</header>
<form  id="searchForm"  role="search"  action="http://search.yahoo.com/
search" method="get">
<label for="q">Search:</label>
<input type="search" id="q" name="q" placeholder="Search..." autofocus
/>
<input type="submit" value="find" />
</form>
<div id="results"></div>
...
</section>
<!-- browse page -->
```

```
<section id="browse" role="region" aria-labelledby="browse">
<header>
<h2 property="alternativeHeadline">Browse the latest items... </h2>
</header>
<ul id="viewObjects"></ul>
...
</section>
<!-- settings page -->
<section id="set" role="region" aria-labelledby="set">
<header>
<h2 property="alternativeHeadline">App Settings</h2>
</header>
<form class="settings" id="settings" action="#set">
<label for="feed">Set feed URL for app</label>
<input type="text" name="feed" id="feed" value="" />
<label for="site">Set site URL for app</label>
<input type="text" name="site" id="site" value="" />
</form>
<p id="message"></p>
<input type="submit" name="save" id="save" value="save" />
<input type="submit" name="clear" id="clear" value="clear" />
</section>
```

Note that each of the <section> elements have an id= attribute with a specific value. The values clearly demarcate the page divisions and we can use these values to create the page view behavior with our JavaScript later in this tutorial.

Step 4: Adding Page View Behavior to the Single-Page Application

With our page structures in place, the next step is to set up the JavaScript that creates the interaction behavior of moving certain HTML <section>s into view based on a user's navigation selection. The script keys on the different <section> id= attributes to create the page view behavior. Let's walk through how that happens. Our first act in the script is to declare the page behavior as a setView function and then to set up the variables used.

```
function setView(name) {
```

```
var name;
var i;
var views = document.getElementsByTagName("section");
if (!name) { name = "#home"; }
```

The function is now open and you can see the name, i, and views variables are declared. The **views** variable has an additional declaration—document.getElementsByTagName—that tells the script to find all the <section> elements on the page and use them as the base value for the variable. This means that all of the <section> values, including id=, will be stored and can be used later. The **if (!name)** sets the default page ID as a **#home** value, ensuring that our default page view for the app will be the home page. The next part of the script turns the views on or off.

```
for (i=0; i<views.length; ++i) {
if (name === "#"+views[i].id) {
views[i].style.display = "block";
} else {
views[i].style.display = "none";
}
}
}
```

This section of the script uses the i variable to iterate through the **views** variables to see which <section> "id=" has been selected. It then places a display style, either **block** or **none**, to make the page section come into view or hide from the screen. The final part of the script checks for the hash value in the URL. The app pivots on these page views based on the URL having a specific #hash value in the URL. For example, **html5-mobile-feed-master/index.html#search** would load the search page view.

```
checkHash = (function() {
var hash;
return function() {
if (window.location.hash !== hash) {
hash = window.location.hash;
setView(hash);
}
}
})();
```

The checkHash function gets the value in the URL using the win-
dow.location.hash and then passes the value of the #hash to our earlier
setView function and the page that has been identified shows up on the
screen. Our final step is to set up the script to periodically check on the
#hash value in the URL and to make sure to turn the script on when the
page loads. You can see those pieces below.

```
function init() {
setInterval(checkHash, 100);
}
//call our init function when the page loads
window.onload = init;
```

Step 5: Add the Feed-Loading Behavior to the Single-Page Application

We use a "load this feed" behavior in two of our page views—the home
page and the browse page—in the application. With this script, we are
able to load an external XML feed, parse the contents of the feed, and
then display the pieces of the feed that we want a user to see on the
page. Here's how the script works. First, we set the URL for the feed
using a global variable.

```
//set global variables, use html5 localStorage if available
if (typeof(Storage) !== 'undefined') {
var feedUrl = window.localStorage.getItem("feedUri");
var siteUrl = window.localStorage.getItem("siteUri");
} else {
var feedUrl = 'https://gdata.youtube.com/feeds/users/msulibrary/uploads?
alt=rss';
var siteUrl = 'http://www.lib.montana.edu';
}
```

Note that you can add your own XML feed URL in the var feedUrl
variable. If you have a specific library feed you want the app to display,
feel free to add it here. The next piece of the script sits inside of the
<section id="home"> tag and will take the var feedUrl value to pass it to
the Google Feeds API to set up our parsing and display routine. (Note:
the <section id="browse"> tag has the same script but uses a broader

scope to bring in all of the feed entries. This is another page view, but it still works in a similar fashion.)

```
<script    type="text/javascript"    src="https://www.google.com/jsapi"></
script>
<script type="text/javascript">
google.load("feeds", "1", {"callback" : showFeed});
function showFeed() {
var feed = new google.feeds.Feed(feedUrl);
feed.setNumEntries(3);
feed.includeHistoricalEntries();
```

The above code calls in the Google Feed API (https://developers.google.com/feed/), a utility script from Google that has all kinds of useful methods for processing and displaying XML feeds. Next, we use the **showFeed** function, which lets us display the feed. You can see the **feedUrl** variable used here, and the global value we set at the top of the page tells the script which feed to use. Finally, we set the number of entries, the listed items in the feed, to display to three with the **feed.setNumEntries(3);** statement. (Note: this is the main difference between the home page and the browse page. The **<section id="browse">** tag contains a unique ID that allows us to use the browse page script to bring in all of the entries related to the browse query.) In the last section of the script, we parse the items in the feed and load them into a display.

```
feed.load(function(result) {
if (!result.error) {
var container = document.getElementById("listView");
for (var i = 0; i < result.feed.entries.length; i++) {
var entry = result.feed.entries[i];
var li = document.createElement("li");
li.innerHTML = '<article><h2><a href="' + entry.link + '">' + entry.title +
'</a></h2><p>' + entry.content + '</p></article>';
container.appendChild(li);
}
} else {
var container = document.getElementById("listView");
container.innerHTML = '<li>No items available. <br /><a href="#set">Set
the feed and site for this app</a>.</li>';
```

```
    }
  });
}
```

With the feed loaded and parsed, we need to create HTML to print out to the page. You can see that happening in the li.innerHTML variable above. Each entry "link," "title," and "content" node is stored and ready for printout. Most importantly, the parsed entries need an HTML container to land within. The <section id="home"> tag has another series of tags that we use to push the script results into the user's view. On the home page, these tags are <ul id="listView"></ul>. With these tags in place, the result of the parsing and display script has a home and the generated <li> tags appear as part of the page view.

Step 6: Add Searching Behavior to the Single-Page Application

Another page view within our application is the ability to filter and search the feed itself. Here we are talking about the <section id="search> series of tags. Within the <section id="search>, we set up the <form> and <div> to talk to our search script and then give the response from the search script a place to store and display the query result.

```
<form id="searchForm" role="search" action="http://search.yahoo.com/
search" method="get">
<label for="q">Search: </label>
<input type="search" id="q" name="q" placeholder="Search" autofocus /
>
<input type="submit" value="find" />
</form>
<div id="results"></div>
```

With the foundational HTML markup in place, we can turn to the search script itself. We are going to use the Yahoo Query Language API (https://developer.yahoo.com/yql/console/), a general means of querying XML feeds and other data sources, to allow us to search across our XML feed. Our script is built using two major functions and an output statement. The query function, the first of the two functions, is below.

```
<script type="text/javascript">
function query(term){
var query = 'select * from feed where url="'+ feedUrl +'" AND title like
"%'+encodeURIComponent(term)+'%" OR url="'+ feedUrl +'" AND descrip-
tion LIKE "%'+encodeURIComponent(term)+'%" | unique(field="link")';
// start the URL by defining the API endpoint and encoding the query
var apiendpoint = 'http://query.yahooapis.com/v1/public/yql?q=';
var url = apiendpoint + encodeURIComponent(query);
// diagnostics - remove if you don't need them
url += '&diagnostics=true';
// format (json or xml)
url += '&format=json';
// callback function (when format is json this triggers JSON-P-X output)
url += '&callback=searchFeed';
// environment. this gives you access to the community tables
url += '&env=store%3A%2F%2Fdatatables.org%2Falltableswithkeys';
var s = document.createElement('script');
s.setAttribute('src',url);
document.getElementsByTagName('head')[0].appendChild(s);
}
```

With this function, we are setting up the variables and the query statement for talking to the Yahoo Query Language API. The var url brings
all of these components together so that we can pass a URL value to the
second function, the searchFeed function.

```
function searchFeed(o){
if(o.query && o.query.results && o.query.results.item){
var res = o.query.results.item,
out = '<ol>',
i = 0,
entry = '';
for(i=0,j=res.length;i<j;i++){
entry = res[i];
out += '<li><h2><a href="'+entry.link+'">'+entry.title+'</a>< h2><p>'
+entry.description+'</p></li>';
}
out += '</ol>';
out += '<p><a href="#search">new search</a><p>';
output.innerHTML = out;
} else {
```

```
output.innerHTML = '<p class="error">No search results. <a href=
"#search">Try another search</a>.</p>';
   }
};
```

This part of the script does most of the heavy lifting. It takes the result value passed from Yahoo Query Language API, parses each entry returned, and then formats the entries as HTML. Finally, we move from the parsing of the API results into the output of the data to the page.

```
var output = document.createElement('div');
output.setAttribute('id','yqldata');
document.getElementById('results').appendChild(output);
var f = document.getElementsByTagName('form')[0];
f.onsubmit = function(){
output.innerHTML = 'Loading&hellip;';
query(document.getElementById('q').value);
return false;
};
</script>
```

Something that might be coming clear is that you always need a place for a user to enter data and for the data results of your script to land and appear. This last section of the script carries out that activity. With the document.getElementByID, the results are being instructed to appear inside of the <div id="results> tag we set up with the initial HTML. And finally, the document.getElementsByTagName is telling the script to use the <form> input on the page to allow the user to pass a query to our feed-parsing script.

Step 7: Add Feed-Settings Behavior to the Single-Page Application

In step 5, we noted that you could set a default XML feed URL for the app to display. Our app also allows for users to enter a feed URL of their choice. This functionality appears on the <section id="set"> tags, the "settings" page view. First, we need the HTML to allow for the interaction.

```
<form class="settings" id="settings" action="#set">
```

```
<label for="feed">Set feed URL for app</label>
<input type="text" name="feed" id="feed" value="" />
<label for="site">Set site URL for app</label>
<input type="text" name="site" id="site" value="" />
</form>
<p id="message"></p>
<input type="submit" name="save" id="save" value="save" />
<input type="submit" name="clear" id="clear" value="clear" />
```

Next, we set up the script that allows the app to receive and store values that the user enters through the form.

```
<script type="text/javascript">
//set variables for app settings routine
var feed = document.getElementById("feed");
var site = document.getElementById("site");
var msg = document.getElementById("message");
//show data from previous edit in form
if (!feed.value) {
feed.value = window.localStorage.getItem('feedUri');
}
if (!site.value) {
site.value = window.localStorage.getItem('siteUri');
}
function saveData() {
window.localStorage.setItem("feedUri", feed.value);
window.localStorage.setItem("siteUri", site.value);
msg.innerHTML = '<strong>Feed and site settings saved. </strong>';
}
function clearData() {
window.localStorage.clear();
document.getElementById("message").innerHTML="";
feed.value = feed.defaultValue;
site.value = site.defaultValue;
msg.innerHTML = '<strong>Feed and site settings cleared. </strong>';
}
//create click events for each form button
document.getElementById("save").onclick = function() { saveData(); return
false;};
document.getElementById("clear").onclick = function() { clearData(); return
false;};
```

```
</script>
```

This is the full script, but you can see the global variables being set in **var feed**, for example. Next, there are some conditional checks to see if there is already a value for the global variables. The most interesting part of the script appears within the **saveData** and **clearData** functions. Here we are using the HTML 5 **localStorage** function to either set and keep a value for the XML feed URL or to clear the value and let the user enter a new XML feed URL. One benefit of the **localStorage** function is that it is stored within the browser and remains until a user clears it. This means that once set, it will still be able to load the last feed that was assigned the next time the app is loaded.

Step 8: Making the Single-Page Application Responsive

Of course, our work here is not complete until we make the app work across multiple devices and platforms. As with most of our other RWD work, we are going to rely on CSS and the media query to make our app appear in different ways according to the size of the screen. If you want to follow along, switch the view in your text editor to the master.css file. Our first step is to zero out the base font size so that we can set reliable breakpoints.

```
body{color:#39444a;font:normal 100%/1.5 'Open Sans',Helvetica,Arial,sans-
serif;}
```

The specific declaration **normal 100%/1.5** tells the Web browser that our later measurement of ems will have size settings of 1 em equaling 16 pixels. This baseline allows us to assign specific rules based on screen size. There are actually four breakpoints for our application. Under the initial **body{}** declarations in the CSS, the default rules of the stylesheet also provide our first responsive look and feel by assigning rules that govern display in desktop and laptop settings. The first actual breakpoint using a media query assignment is for large screens.

```
@media only screen and (min-width: 75.750em) {
```

In the rules within this CSS media query, we allow our app to stretch out and utilize as much screen space as possible. It also sets a two-column layout and allows our image to adjust to screen real estate. Our next media query sets up a breakpoint for small tablets and large smartphones.

```
@media only screen and (max-width: 47.938em) and (min-width:
30.000em) {
```

The rules within this media query introduce a one-column layout and shrink the size of the image to allow for it to fit on the screen. The primary new rule in this media query is the **body{}** and the **#doc{}** declarations.

```
body {width:396px;-webkit-text-size-adjust:100%;padding:10px 42px 0;}
#doc > div,#doc > footer,#doc > aside {float:none;clear:none;}
```

With the body width set to less than 400 pixels and the floats removed, the layout starts to move horizontally and become a series of linear blocks stacked on top of one another. The final breakpoint is for standard smartphones.

```
@media only screen and (max-width: 29.938em) {
```

The series of rules within this breakpoint hide the image, remove extraneous margins and padding, and shrink the viewport to around 290 pixels.

```
body {width:290px;-webkit-text-size-adjust:100%;font-size:13px;
line-height:18px;margin:0 auto;padding:10px;}
...
#doc > aside img {display:none;}
```

With this final set of rules, the app displays seamlessly on common smartphones, and this project is complete. Once you are satisfied with the changes, make sure all your open files are saved and then move the whole folder from the template app (with all your customizations and edits) to a public Web directory.

5.6 USING AN RWD FRAMEWORK FOR A COMPLETE SITE—TWITTER BOOTSTRAP

View the demo:
www.lib.montana.edu/~jason/files/rwd-bootstrap/
Download the files:
https://github.com/jasonclark/rwd-bootstrap/
  or
www.lib.montana.edu/~jason/files/rwd-bootstrap.zip

Web design and development has become a complex business. Beyond the complexity of designing for multiple screens, consider just some of the questions that a developer or designer has to think about:

- What database store might work best for my data?
- Which programming language gives me the most flexibility to parse or display my data?
- What types of typographic styles and display styles communicate my brand most effectively?
- How might my user interface fit within the common expectations for how Web applications work?

Let me be clear that I'm not complaining. This complexity is not necessarily bad. It has forced developers and designers to look at the common elements of Web applications and to build shortcuts and create libraries of code that give us a head start. More specifically, the complexity has given rise to front-end frameworks composed of CSS snippets, HTML markup, and JavaScript functions that answer common design patterns and conventional user interface components. There really is no shortage to these frameworks and some of the most popular include the HTML5 Boilerplate (https://html5boilerplate.com/), Foundation (http://foundation.zurb.com/), and Bootstrap (http://getbootstrap.com/) from the development team at Twitter.com. For this project we create a complete, prototype Web site for a fictional library, including a home page, about page, contact page, and search page. We are using Bootstrap (version 3.0) to get us started due to its popularity and because responsive design has been "baked in" Bootstrap since version 2.0. The goal is to get familiar with the Bootstrap framework and to get started on a possible redesign or rethinking of your Web site. The result is a responsively designed Web site that works across multiple platforms and screen sizes.

Step 1: Download the Bootstrap Template Files

As mentioned in the introduction, we are downloading a working, prototype Web site and explaining the code that makes the site work. I have added and refined the Bootstrap framework code to provide a set of starter template files. You can get the customized files at www.lib.montana.edu/~jason/files/rwd-bootstrap.zip. Unzip the files and open up the following files in your text editor.

- index.html
- /css/master.css

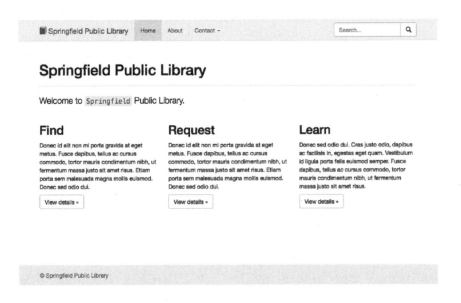

Figure 5.18. Bootstrap Page on Large Screen, Springfield Library Home Page

Figure 5.19. Bootstrap Page on Small Screen, Springfield Library Home Page

Step 2: Activating the Bootstrap Framework on All of the Site Pages

Our first step in setting up the foundation of the site begins with the <head> tag on the index.html file, which identifies the main CSS styles and the name for the page. Add the name that you want for the page in between the <title> tags.

```
<head>
<meta charset="utf-8">
<meta http-equiv="X-UA-Compatible" content="IE=edge">
<meta name="viewport" content="width=device-width, initial-scale=1">
<meta name="description" content="">
```

```
<meta name="author" content="">
<link rel="icon" href="./favicon.ico">
<title>Springfield Public Library - RWD Example</title>
<!-- Bootstrap core CSS -->
<link href="./css/bootstrap.min.css" rel="stylesheet">
<!-- Custom styles for this template -->
<link href="./css/master.css" rel="stylesheet">
<!-- HTML5 shim and Respond.js for IE8 support of HTML5 elements and
media queries -->
<!--[if lt IE 9]>
<script src="https://oss.maxcdn.com/html5shiv/3.7.2/html5shiv.min.js"></
script>
<script    src="https://oss.maxcdn.com/respond/1.4.2/respond.min.js"></
script>
<![endif]-->
</head>
```

The code above brings in the look and feel of the site. One of the advantages of the Bootstrap framework is the well-conceived and cross-browser tested CSS rules that create a clean look and feel for our typography and layout. You can see these rules are now in place with the <link href="./css/bootstrap.min.css" rel="stylesheet"> line. Custom styles that we might add to our site are added using the following line: <link href="./css/master.css" rel="stylesheet">. These links to stylesheets appear on all of our pages in the project. The second part of this step involves setting up the core JavaScript that allows us to make our pages behave in certain ways and responsively adapt to different screens and platforms. Near the bottom of the index.html file are the following lines.

```
<!-- Bootstrap core JavaScript ===========================
========================= -->
<!-- Placed at the end of the document so the pages load faster -->
<script src="https://ajax.googleapis.com/ajax/libs/jquery/1.11.1/jquery.min.
js"></script>
<script src="./js/bootstrap.min.js"></script>
<!-- IE10 viewport hack for Surface/desktop Windows 8 bug -->
<script src="./js/ie10-viewport-bug-workaround.js"></script>
</body>
```

It should be clear by now that we activate the Bootstrap framework by linking and referencing certain files such as jQuery (another JavaScript library upon which Bootstrap is dependent) and bootstrap.min.js. Each page created using Bootstrap has these lines. With this project, the files are about.html, contact.html, index.html, and search.html. Open all of the remaining files (with the exception of index.html) in your text editor and verify that the lines are present.

Step 3: Understanding the HTML Foundations of the Bootstrap Framework—Navigation Bar

With the baseline CSS and JavaScript in place, the next step is crafting the HTML markup that forms the page sections of the Web site. Bootstrap uses specific conventions and class identifiers in its HTML markup to make certain page behaviors and page displays happen, and in this step we'll look at what this markup is. Starting with the index.html file again, we see a specific set of HTML markup as the <body> tag opens.

```
<!-- Fixed navbar -->
<nav class="navbar navbar-default navbar-fixed-top">
<div class="container">
<div class="navbar-header">
<button type="button" class="navbar-toggle collapsed" data-toggle=
"collapse"    data-target="#navbar"    aria-expanded="false"    aria-con-
trols="navbar">
<span class="sr-only">Toggle navigation</span>
<span class="icon-bar"></span>
<span class="icon-bar"></span>
<span class="icon-bar"></span>
</button>
<a class="navbar-brand" href="index.html">
<span    class="glyphicon    glyphicon-book"    aria-hidden="true"></span>
Springfield Public Library</a>
</div>
<div id="navbar" class="collapse navbar-collapse">
<ul class="nav navbar-nav">
<li class="active"><a href="index.html">Home</a></li>
<li class="dropdown">
<a    href="#"    class="dropdown-toggle"    data-toggle="dropdown"    role=
"button" aria-expanded="false">Contact <span class="caret"
```

```
></span></a>
<ul class="dropdown-menu" role="menu">
<li><a href="contact.html">Contact form</a></li>
<li><a href="contact.html#phone">Phone</a></li>
<li><a href="contact.html#address">Address</a></li>
</ul>
</li>
</ul>
<ul class="nav navbar-nav navbar-right">
<li>
<form    class="navbar-form"    role="search"    method="get"    action=
"search.html">
<div class="input-group">
<input id="q" name="q" type="text" class="form-control" placeholder=
"Search...">
<div class="input-group-btn">
<button class="btn btn-default" type="submit">
<i class="glyphicon glyphicon-search"></i></button> </div>
</div>
</form>
</li>
</ul>
</div><!--/.nav-collapse -->
</div>
</nav>
```

The above markup is our navigation bar, which appears on all of our pages. You can see it in figure 5.20, which shows our about page with the navigation bar at the top.

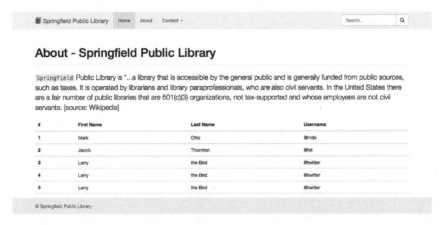

Figure 5.20. Bootstrap "Navbar" Component on Large Screen, About Page

The navigation bar is a central element for our site, and an additional feature is the capability of the Bootstrap framework to make the navigation work on small screens.

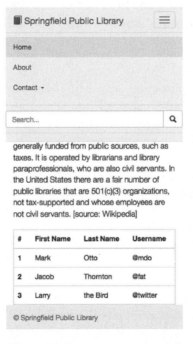

Figure 5.21. Bootstrap "Navbar" Component on Small Screen, About Page

As you can see, the navigation shrinks in these smaller settings and a user can click on the "hamburger" (three stacked lines) icon to make an overlay of the navigation appear. This behavior is inherent to the framework and also one of its most important when creating a responsive Web design. The markup that enables this behavior is:

```
<button   type="button"   class="navbar-toggle   collapsed"   data-tog-
gle="collapse"   data-target="#navbar"   aria-expanded="false"   aria-con-
trols="navbar">
<span class="sr-only">Toggle navigation</span>
```

Remember our Bootstrap core JavaScript from step 2. The boot-strap.min.js script works to push our navigation elements into this col-lapsed navbar so that it can be displayed on small screens. This is where the power of Bootstrap starts to become apparent. You get this type of functionality right out of the box. As a final part of this step, check to make sure the navigation bar appears in the other site files.

Step 4: Understanding the HTML Foundations of the Bootstrap Framework—Content Container and Footer

With our page navigation bar in place, the next step is to set up the content container and footer for all of our pages. As we saw earlier, Bootstrap relies on particular sets of HTML markup and the content pane (where the primary parts of our Web page appear); the footer follows similar markup rules. To create the content container, we use the following markup in the index.html file.

```
<!-- Begin page content -->
<div class="container">
<div class="page-header">
<h1>Springfield Public Library</h1>
</div>
...
</div><!--/.container -->
```

In this case, the container class lets the Bootstrap CSS file know how to display the content and how to flow between screen sizes. In the in-dex.html file, you can also see some markup that allows a developer to take advantage of the built-in grid layout system (http://getboot-strap.com/css/#grid).

```
<div class="row">
<div class="col-md-4">
...
</div
</div>
```

This type of row markup, when paired with three "col-md-4" <div>s, creates a perfect three-column layout that slides into a single-column layout on small screens. The final note in this step is the formation of our footer element. You can see our site footer at the bottom of our contact page.

The markup to make the footer depends on the following HTML code block.

```
<footer class="footer navbar-default navbar-fixed-bottom">
<div class="container">
<p class="text-muted">&copy; Springfield Public Library</p>
</div>
</footer>
```

The </footer> and <div class="container"> markup appear on all of our pages. Note that we have fixed or "pinned" the footer to the bottom of the screen viewport using the "navbar-fixed-bottom" class. This allows the content container to have a separate scroll window and gives our site an

Figure 5.22. Bootstrap Page on Large Screen, Contact Page

app-like feel, as many apps work with fixed headers and footers. As a final check in this step, verify that the </footer> and <div class="container"> markup appears in each of our site pages.

Step 5: Finalizing the CSS Styles

As a rule, you should try to use as many of the default styles that are part of the bootstrap.min.css core CSS. The framework has just about every style you can think of at http://getbootstrap.com/css/. Following this rule also gives consistency to your interface and the most widely supported set of rules for layout and design. Of course, there are always exceptions where you might want to introduce your own layout rule or look and feel. My advice is to tread lightly. In working with the framework, I was pleasantly surprised with the range of styles and user interface components that were available. In step 1, we opened a master.css file. This is the file where we can add enhanced styles and layout customizations to our Web site pages. Note that for these styles to work they need to be called into our pages after the bootstrap.min.css file.

```
/* Custom page CSS ------------------------------------------------ */
/* Not required for template or sticky footer method. */
body > .container {padding:60px 15px 0;}
.container .text-muted {margin:20px 0;}
.footer > .container {padding-right:15px;padding-left:15px; }
code {font-size:80%;}
.form-group.required label:after {content:" *";color:red;}
.top-buffer {margin-top:10px;}
/* Sticky footer method -------------------------------------------- */
.footer.navbar-default.navbar-fixed-bottom {background-color:#f5f5f5;
padding:1em 0;}
.footer.navbar-default.navbar-fixed-bottom  p {margin:0; } body {padding-
bottom:60px;
/*padding behind bottom navbar to allow for scroll*/ }
/* Responsive table styles ----------------------------------------- */
@-moz-document url-prefix() {fieldset {display:table-cell;} }
```

The few customizations in place here are related to making sure our footer stays fixed to the bottom of the viewport. There is a top-buffer class to add extra top padding to elements when extra white space is required. You can see this effect in place on our search page, as the media objects in the search result item list needed extra spacing beyond the default Bootstrap settings.

With these final styles applied, we have completed the walkthrough of our Bootstrap site. Now that you have a basic understanding of the framework as it was applied in this case, you should be able to modify and edit the site to match your local Web site needs. Have fun.

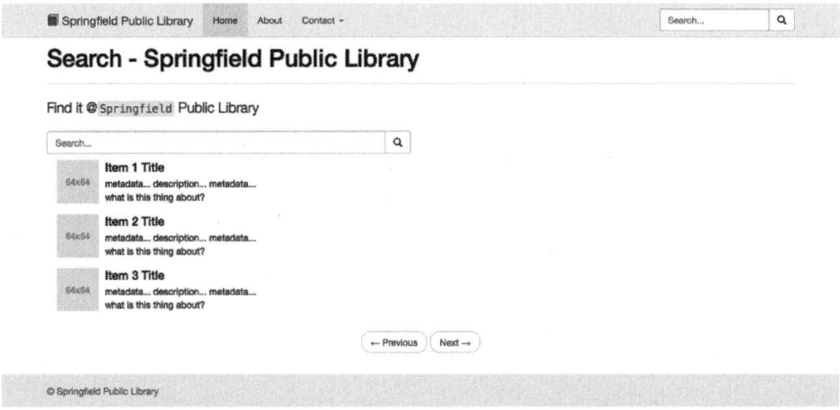

Figure 5.23. Bootstrap Page on Large Screen, Search Page

6

TIPS AND TRICKS

Responsive Web Design (RWD) in Practice

6.1 PRINCIPLES AND TIPS FOR RWD THINKING

In the introduction to this book, I called RWD a groundbreaking theory (at the time that it was introduced by Ethan Marcotte). It is, and it was. RWD has reached the point where it has moved beyond theory into practice; every theory is looking for a way to be put into practice. It happened rapidly for RWD, but there are a number of ways of thinking that allowed that transition to happen. In this chapter, I work through the tips and ways of thinking that allow us to practice RWD. Think of it as a kind of "first principles" of RWD. Okay, maybe that is a bit grand. With the *Principia*, Newton was trying to establish a mathematical way of thinking about natural philosophy, but his practice of establishing a set of rules to promote a way of thinking does work as a frame for this chapter. What does it take to have an RWD mind-set? How do we practice responsive design thinking? We'll answer these questions and others as we try to ground RWD as the way of thinking about development and design.

Principle 1: All Users Deserve the Same Content and Experience

One of the first tips to understand RWD is how the model itself blows away the idea of special context and user needs. There is no mobile-only context; no special things happen when browsing on a laptop. There is simply user experience and a need to ensure that the content is there. Certainly context matters, but RWD forces us to consider how the interaction layer we build needs to work for all. We are serving a single, foundational HTML design that can adapt to the requirements of the moment. This is a huge change, and it means that your site's appearance and visual structure can and will change without ever losing content or functionality for users on any device or screen size.

Principle 2: Breakpoints Are about Content, Not Devices

Breakpoints, those decision points that we code into our design to switch context and appearance, need to be connected to breaks in content display, not just screen size. Screen size is a useful metaphor and mathematical value for the CSS rule we apply to the media query, but the value is not how we should envision how the design should work. Readers or users and their requirements for how the content is most usable or readable is our guiding principle here. This is a different (and at times, a subjective way) of looking at breakpoints, but it allows us to have flexibility as new screens and devices become design patterns. Think in terms of small, medium, and large content needs for your users. Read your content and resize your browser. When things start to look crowded or some of the initial meaning is lost, that is your break-point.

Principle 3: Think in Terms of Modules, Not Page Elements

RWD breaks the page metaphor we have used for the Web since its inception. We tend to think of composite, complete Web pages, but RWD asks us to look at the components of a page as modal actions. Navigation and linking, identity and branding, search and search re-sults; the reading view or pane, metadata and copyright sections, the browsable list—all of these components are modules that can appear anywhere in the flow of our design depending on the small, medium, or large spectrum for device and screen. It's this atomic view that changes the page metaphor. The semantic HTML5 elements help frame this change—<header>, <main>, <aside>, <footer>—these are more closely aligned with concepts than page elements. Keeping these concepts in mind as you are building your code is helpful and necessary as you start RWD.

Principle 4: Flow Is the Primary Action of RWD

The RWD model centers on fluidity. It calls exclusively for flexible media and fluid layout practices. RWD practitioners speak of the flow of content between breakpoints. This action is primary when working at any stage in RWD. With flow in mind, the practice of design and development becomes an act of assigning relative and relational widths and heights on your site components. In practice, this means using relative units like percentages or ems in your CSS rules to set the widths or heights of your HTML tags. A <main> tag might have the corresponding CSS i: main {display:block;width:100%;}. And an <img> tag might have CSS rules that look like img {height:auto;width:100%;max-width:100%;}.

Principle 5: Performance Is Your Metric for User Experience

With an emphasis on a single set of HTML, CSS, and JavaScript files for your design, RWD can lead to pages with large file sizes. Additionally, you have the problem of image files that are best served on the desktop. How users experience your RWD site is a central concern: performance is a metric for trust and a marker of good design. And the way forward is to optimize your files to load fast. For text files like HTML, CSS, and JavaScript, there are methods like minification and compression that can help reduce file size. Utilities like HTML Minifier (www.willpeavy.com/minifier/) are helpful here. There are similar methods for keeping images and media in check. See Smush.it (www.smushit.com/ysmush.it/). But beyond these compression techniques, you can also think about setting performance budgets. Take, for example, this type of requirement based on average expectations for page load times: "This site must load on a smartphone on an edge network in less than 1.5 seconds" (www.nytimes.com/2012/03/01/tech-nology/impatient-web-users-flee-slow-loading-sites.html).

Principle 6: Drop the Mouse Interaction Model and Design Pattern

The age of precision pointing and clicking is over. Increasingly, our users are working in touch environments, and it's almost impossible to forecast what other interaction patterns and interface elements might emerge. This means that the way we design our actions (think links and buttons) needs to change. These interface components need extra padding and large targets for thumbs. It also means the events and behaviors we assign via our scripts and CSS rules to these components need to become more generic as well. Common CSS rules like a:hover that make links change based on a mouse cursor hovering over a link do not work in touch environments. Similarly, the common JavaScript events onmouseover or hover-based actions are not long for this design world. New JavaScript events that work across devices, such as onblur or onfocus, are becoming the new standards. The key is to broaden your understanding of the design language and look at ways to build interface components without the mouse in mind.

Principle 7: Create Reusable and Portable Data

The next principle is almost defensive in nature. It follows from the idea that we can't always be sure how or when our content is viewed or consumed. It might be inside a Google search result, a Twitter time line, on an Apple watch, or even interpreted by a machine trying to classify what your page is about. Think of your RWD site as a data source. Build your RWD site with the idea that your content might be shared, parsed for meaning, or even reused as open data. This means designing rich markup that has meaning for machines and people using Schema.org, a Web classification language for defining the properties of your site (http://schema.org/). It also might mean adding OpenGraph protocol (http://ogp.me/) tags to allow your site or pages to be understood in social media settings like Facebook. The goal is to engineer for reuse and portability and to allow for the chance that your data might be decoupled from your Web presentation. This type of thinking might enable your site to appear on that smart refrigerator screen or the self-driving car dashboard of the near future.

Principle 8: Set Up Your RWD Metrics and Define What Success Looks Like

The final principle is one of the most important: you need to define what a successful implementation of RWD entails. Is it sticky pages? Is it people browsing the site even when on small screens? There are analytics packages that can help you understand how your RWD site is working, Google Analytics being one of the most popular (www.google.com/analytics/). Within these tools, there are common filters to watch and build analytics reports around, including device category, operating system, operating system version, browser, and browser version. With these filters in place, you can get specific views of device and browser and start to analyze where your users are. But that still doesn't define the success metric. Some common measures of RWD performance might be watching for high bounce rates (i.e., are people loading and leaving immediately?). Another metric to measure against are page load times. You want all devices loading pages quickly and efficiently. Finally, measure and think about a benchmark around "time on page" metrics such as pages per session (visit) or session duration (time on site).

7

FUTURE TRENDS

Responsive Web Design (RWD)

7.1 WHAT'S ON THE HORIZON FOR RWD

Fluid grids, flexible images and objects, and media queries are the three core components for responsive Web design, and these components have served developers well in the five years since Ethan Marcotte introduced the RWD model. But responsive design is still in its morning phase. With RWD emerging as the dominant Web design and development model, we are starting to see standards bodies like the World Wide Web Consortium (W3C: www.w3.org/) and working groups like the Web Hypertext Application Technology Working Group (WHATWG: https://whatwg.org/) introduce new HTML elements and CSS rules that answer some common RWD problems. The latest Web browsers are starting to implement these changes in some of their alpha and beta releases. In this chapter, I take a closer look at some of these new developments and track where RWD appears to be going. It is worth mentioning that many of these HTML, CSS, and JavaScript additions are bleeding edge. Be sure to check HTML5 Please (http:// html5please.com/) for questions on implementation and browser support.

New HTML Markup for Images

From the beginning of our RWD implementations, we have been aware of a major performance issue: images. That is, we have taken great care to shape our layouts and typography with media queries but have sent the same large images created for desktop screens to even the smallest screen, letting these devices choke and hiccup as they try to display them on limited screen real estate and with limited network connections. With this in mind, W3C has introduced two new HTML elements: the **srcset** attribute for the <img> tag and the <picture> tag. The solution behind these elements is simple: send a specific, optimized image depending on context and device. An **srcset** attribute allows us to offer multiple versions of an image to browsers with an assigned size that enables the browser to pick the most appropriate image to load. Here's a quick example of an image tag using the **srcset** attribute:

```
<img
srcset="http://covers.openlibrary.org/b/isbn/0385472579-L.jpg 1920w,
http://covers.openlibrary.org/b/isbn/0385472579-M.jpg 960w,
http://covers.openlibrary.org/b/isbn/0385472579-S.jpg 480w"
sizes="(min-width:800px) 50vw,100vw"
src=" http://covers.openlibrary.org/b/isbn/0385472579-M.jpg"
alt="Book cover image for Zen Speaks by Tsi Chih Chung" />
```

Note that this is using a standard image tag with an **src** attribute that will work in every browser. Newer browsers pick up new attributes and serve the optimized image. The new **srcset** attribute has a value listing the location of the image along with the width descriptor that lets the browser know the width dimensions of the image. We also define the min-width via a media query in the **sizes** attribute to set a baseline for the display with the **min-width:800px) 50vw,100vw** expression using the new viewport unit measurement (which I discuss in the next section). With this info in the page, the browser does the rest of the work in determining which image to use and display. The <picture> tag follows a similar approach by stacking any number of source elements and one img inside its opening and closing tags.

```
<picture>
<source media="(orientation: landscape)" srcset="http://covers.openlibrary
.org/b/isbn/0385472579-L.jpg" />
```

```
<source media="(min-width: 500px)" srcset="http://covers.openlibrary.org/
b/isbn/0385472579-S.jpg" />
<img  src="http://covers.openlibrary.org/b/isbn/0385472579-M.jpg"  alt=
"Book cover image for Zen Speaks by Tsi Chih Chung" />
</picture>
```

The browser looks at the source and image elements until it finds one whose media attribute matches the current device and screen display. Both of the elements are looking to solve the same problem, and like many of these new, emerging RWD trends, the one that will become the standard depends on browser implementation and developer uptake.

New CSS Styles and Rules for Precision

With the multiplicity of devices and screens continuing to grow, developers are in need of different ways to describe measurements and to check for support of various elements that depend on certain screen sizes. This is the pressure of RWD coming to bear on CSS. Standards bodies and browser implementations have created some new options to address this pressure. The viewport unit—vh, vw, vmin, vmax—is a measurement unit that allows elements to be sized proportionally to the browser's viewport. A vh is 1/100 of the viewport's height, a vw is 1/100 of the viewport's width, and vmin and vmax are 1/100 of whichever dimension is smaller or larger, respectively. You saw how we could use these units earlier when we set a baseline size for our image using the (min-width:800px) 50vw,100vw expression. In this case, we were setting our image to be sized within one-half of the browser's viewport if the browser window is wider than 800 pixels, and if it's smaller than 800 pixels, it'll probably be full-width. Viewport units allow us to create unique queries of viewport values that could be retrieved and measured only by JavaScript before, and they can be applied to layout measurements (not just images). It gives us a new, accurate tool to build responsive designs with precision targeting and behaviors for just about any device or screen. The @viewport, light-level media query, and @supports rules are two other CSS additions that can help us out. The <meta name="viewport" has always been a bit of a hack, as it is an HTML tag tied directly to a display setting. With the @viewport rule, we now have

the same viewport control we have with the meta tag but within the CSS, where we control layout, typography, and all presentational look and feel for our pages. An example CSS declaration for **@viewport** will look like this:

```
@viewport {
width: device-width;
zoom: 1;
}
```

Using **width:device-width** tells the page to find and match the screen's width. Once this match is made, it allows the page to adapt content to match different screen sizes. The **zoom:1** property defines the initial scale of the page and the zoom level. This level of control is essential as the viewport rule is how we trigger our media queries, and it makes complete sense to place the rule alongside our other layout and display directives in a CSS file. Along similar lines, there is an early "environment media features" specification in CSS4 to allow media queries to trigger based on light levels (http://dev.w3.org/csswg/mediaqueries-4/). Once implemented, it allows you to check for ambient light and adapt your design accordingly. A sample of this rule might look like this:

```
@media (light-level: dim) {
/* ADD YOUR LOW LIGHT, HIGH-CONTRAST STYLES */
}
```

Finally, we have the **@supports** rule, which gives us the chance to do feature detection to check whether a device or screen had certain CSS properties that we could use as developers. Here's a test for flexbox support (a new layout style that I talk about next) using the **@supports** rule:

```
@supports (display: flex) {
div { display: flex; }
}
```

The rules inside the **@supports** expression are only applied if the conditions are met. Developers could carry out this conditional expression and testing using only JavaScript in the past and having this logic inside our CSS is advantageous for RWD settings.

New Layout Styles and JavaScript APIs for Performance

Building a flexible grid has always been problematic. When developing within an RWD model, we have a common need to move between columned and linear layouts. A number of layout solutions and models have been proposed, but one of the most promising is flexbox (https://developer.mozilla.org/en-US/docs/Web/Guide/CSS/Flexible_boxes). The flexible box model makes columns and grids fairly simple. We can take simple collections of <div>s below and wrap it in a flex container.

```
<div class="flex">
<div>box 1</div>
<div>box 2</div>
<div>box 3</div>
</div>
```

In this case the flex container is the <div class="flex"> element. By adding the following styles, we can set the container into a row of three boxes that flows into a single column of three boxes as the screen gets smaller.

```
.flex {
width: 90%;
height: 200px;
/* flexbox setup */
display: -webkit-flex;
-webkit-flex-direction: row;
display: flex;
flex-direction: row;
}
.flex > div {
-webkit-flex: 1 1 auto;
flex: 1 1 auto;
width: 30px;
-webkit-transition: width 0.7s ease-out;
transition: width 0.7s ease-out;
}
```

I'm going quickly over this layout mode, but it has the potential to make RWD layouts simple and it is worth watching. To get a sense of how more complex layout questions can be answered, check out "Solved by Flexbox" (http://philipwalton.github.io/solved-by-flexbox/).

Beyond the flexible box model, there are a number of new additions that consider how to improve performance and speed of RWD sites. For example, matchMedia provides a JavaScript API to see if a media query will succeed. You can use the matchMedia.js JavaScript polyfill (https://github.com/paulirish/matchMedia.js/) to help older browsers use the API. (A polyfill is a script, usually JavaScript, that you can link to in your page that tells browsers how to use some of these bleeding-edge functions and APIs.) A common expression using the matchMedia API could look like this:

```
if (matchMedia('all and (orientation:landscape)').matches) {
/* probably tablet in widescreen view */
}
```

Using this kind of expression, you could target rules for a tablet in a widescreen view. Without APIs like this, there would be no way to carry out RWD with any kind of precision. We can also see a theme of improving performance coming through with these experimental new features. The Network Information API monitors and reports on the status and type of connection a device or computer is using (network, cellular, Wi-Fi, Bluetooth, etc.). With this information in hand, developers can make dynamic changes to the RWD pages and inform the user that the network connection type has changed. All of these emerging features point to a different kind of RWD that some have called adaptive Web design (AWD). The idea is to engineer a smarter RWD model where only the elements that are needed are sent to the browser and device. With this AWD technological model, many of the decisions regarding which HTML, CSS, and JavaScript snippets or files to send to a user on a device will happen on the server. A corollary design movement is called RESS (responsive Web design + server side components). The goal is to provide snappy interfaces and to require the download of only the pieces of the RWD site that are needed (www.lukew.com/ff/entry.asp?1392). It is a move toward understanding context and building responsively using that context. Whatever the name, AWD or RESS, it is a performance trend and design model worth watching as we move into the next generation of RWD.

RECOMMENDED READING
Responsive Web Design (RWD) in Practice

8.1 LINKS, RESOURCES, AND READINGS FOR RWD

This collection of Web sites, books, and other resources will help you stay on top of the RWD conversation and will point you to useful development resources as you start to put the ideas from this book into practice. Since RWD is an evolving field, I plan to keep a live linkroll of useful resources related to this book at https://pinboard.in/u:jasonclark/t:rwd-in-practice/. Bookmark the URL and check it regularly, as I'll continue to post items to the "rwd-in-practice" tag when I find something new and relevant.

Background, History, and Context for RWD

A good place to start is at the beginning with Ethan Marcotte's book. As the RWD model has evolved, Scott Jehl has some great advice on performance and new metrics for RWD success.

Marcotte, Ethan. *Responsive Web Design*. New York: A Book Apart, 2011.
Jehl, Scott, and Ethan Marcotte. *Responsible Responsive Design*. New York: A Book Apart, 2014.

In addition, Jason Griffey's study of mobile technology in libraries provides some important history and context for our institutions.

Griffey, Jason. *Mobile Technology and Libraries*. Chicago: Neal-Schuman Publishers, 2010.

Tagwatching is another useful means of gathering information related to your topic of interest. Tagwatching involves choosing a service or Web site, finding a relevant tag, and then watching or monitoring the tag in a feedreader or Web browser. Here are a few examples to get you started.

- www.smashingmagazine.com/tag/responsive-web-design/
- http://pinboard.in/t:rwd/
- http://pinboard.in/t:responsive-design/
- http://stackoverflow.com/questions/tagged/responsive-design/

Tutorials

There are a number of tutorials that provide good information and walkthroughs in applying RWD. I have highlighted a few resources below from some of my favorite reputable sources.

Creating a Mobile-First Responsive Web Design—HTML5 Rocks: www.html5rocks.com/en/mobile/responsivedesign/

Beginner's Guide to Responsive Design—Treehouse: http://blog.teamtreehouse.com/beginners-guide-to-responsive-web-design

UI Design Guidelines for Responsive Design—Codrops: http://tympanus.net/codrops/2013/01/21/ui-design-guidelines-for-responsive-design/

Responsive Web Design: What It Is and How to Use It—Smashing Magazine: www.smashingmagazine.com/2011/01/12/guidelines-for-responsive-web-design/

Responsive Web Design Basics—Google Developers: https://developers.google.com/web/fundamentals/layouts/rwd-fundamentals/

Fluid Layouts and Media Queries

The concepts behind fluid layouts and media queries can be difficult to understand. Here are a few resources that define the terms and give some suggestions for implementation and future directions.

Fluid Grids—A List Apart: http://alistapart.com/article/fluidgrids

CSS Media Queries—Mozilla Developer Network: https://developer.mozilla.org/en-US/docs/Web/Guide/CSS/Media_queries

Determining Breakpoints for a Responsive Design—Creative Bloq: www.creativebloq.com/responsive-web-design/determining-breakpoints-responsive-design-8122871

Media Queries: http://mediaqueri.es/

Flexible Media and Objects

Finding ways to make traditionally fixed or static objects flexible is a requirement for RWD. The resources below show how that can be accomplished and explain the reason behind this technique.

Which Responsive Image Technique Should I Use?—CSS Tricks: https://css-tricks.com/which-responsive-images-solution-should-you-use/

Creating Intrinsic Ratios for Video—A List Apart: http://alistapart.com/article/creating-intrinsic-ratios-for-video

Responsive HTML5 Video—Ian Devlin: www.iandevlin.com/blog/2012/08/html5/responsive-html5-video

Optimization and Performance

With the RWD model calling for a single HTML file and producing large CSS files, it is worth the time to optimize and compress the pages for performance. The resources below provide some guidance and point to some utilities for optimization.

Optimizing Responsive Design Websites for Performance—Sitepoint: www.sitepoint.com/optimizing-responsive-design-websites-for-performance/

You May Be Losing Users If Responsive Web Design Is Your Only Mobile Strategy: www.smashingmagazine.com/2014/07/22/responsive-web-design-should-not-be-your-only-mobile-strategy/

Page Speed Insights—Minifying Resources: https://developers.google.com/speed/docs/insights/MinifyResources

Future of RWD

As I have mentioned throughout the book, RWD is a rapidly evolving field with all kinds of possible futures. The resources below try to map our what that future might hold.

The Next Big Thing in Responsive Design: www.fastcodesign.com/3036091/the-next-big-thing-in-responsive-design

Surveying the Big Screen—A List Apart: http://alistapart.com/article/surveying-the-big-screen

Moving beyond the Responsive Web to the Adaptive Web—Sitepoint: www.sitepoint.com/moving-beyond-responsive-web-adaptive-web/

INDEX

ABOUT THE AUTHOR

Jason A. Clark is head of Library Informatics & Computing, where he builds and directs the digital branch of the Montana State University (MSU) library. In his work, he has focused on semantic Web development, digital library development, metadata and data modeling, Web services and APIs, search engine optimization, and interface design.

Before coming to MSU in 2005, Jason became interested in the intersection between libraries and technology while working as a Web developer for the Division of Information Technology at the University of Wisconsin. After two years, he moved on to the Web services department at Williams College libraries. When he doesn't have metadata on the brain, he likes to hike the mountains of Montana with his wife, Jennifer, their daughter, Piper, and their dog, Oakley.

You can find Jason online by following him on twitter at twitter.com/ jaclark or by checking out his occasional thoughts and code samples on his Web site at www.jasonclark.info.